HOT PUDDINGS, SOUFFLÉS, & FRITTERS

Domestic Art Series

By FLORENCE B. JACK

AUTHOR OF THE "ART OF LAUNDRY WORK,"
"COOKING FOR INVALIDS," ETC. ETC.

Creative Cookbooks
Monterrey, California

Hot Puddings, Souffles, & Fritters

by
Florence B. Jack

ISBN: 1-58963-376-8

Reprinted from the 1905 edition

Creative Cookbooks
An Imprint of Fredonia Books
Monterey, California
http://www.creativecookbooks.com

CONTENTS.

———◆———

INDEX.

IMPERIAL WEIGHTS AND MEASURES.

Avoirdupois Weight.

16 drachms (dr.) - - -	make 1	ounce (oz.).
16 ounces - - •	„ 1	pound (lb.).
28 pounds - • •	„ 1	quarter (qr.).
4 quarters - • •	„ 1	hundredweight(cwt.)
20 hundredweights -	„ 1	ton.

14 pounds - • •	make 1	stone.
8 stones • • •	„ 1	hundredweight.
112 pounds - • •	„ 1	hundredweight.

Liquid Measure of Capacity.

4 gills - • - -	make 1	pint (pt.).
2 pints - • • •	„ 1	quart (qrt.).
4 quarts • • •	„ 1	gallon (gal.).

Dry Measure of Capacity.

2 gallons • - -	make 1	peck (pk.).
4 pecks · • •	„ 1	bushel (bush.).
8 bushels • • -	„ 1	quarter (qr.).

HOMELY MEASURES.

2 teaspoonfuls - -	make 1	dessertspoonful.
2 dessertspoonfuls -	„ 1	tablespoonful.
1 heaped tablespoonful of solids - -	„	about 1 ounce.
1 teacupful of solids -	„	about ¼ lb.
1 teacupful of liquid -	„	fully 1 gill.
1 tumblerful of liquid -	„	about ½ pint.

HOT PUDDINGS, SOUFFLÉS, AND FRITTERS.

GENERAL NOTES ON PUDDING MAKING.

THE word "pudding" has a somewhat comprehensive meaning, used as often as not to signify any sweet dish whatever.

The class of preparations known as puddings is very varied, comprising milk puddings, suet and custard puddings, batter pudding mixtures, cake-like mixtures, soufflés, and pastry of different kinds.

Before beginning to make a pudding, gather together all the materials necessary, and weigh or measure everything carefully.

If trying a recipe for the first time, read it carefully through from the beginning to the end.

Then consider the manner in which the pudding has to be cooked.

If a baked pudding, see that the oven is at the right degree of heat.

Milk puddings require a moderate oven. Any pudding of the nature of a soufflé and pastry require a hot oven.

Custard puddings, and all those containing custard, must be slowly cooked. A pudding to be steamed must be put into a well-greased mould or basin, and covered over with a piece of buttered paper. If a steamer is not available for the purpose, put the pudding into a stewpan with just sufficient water to come half-way up the mould, put the lid on the pan, and keep the water at simmering point until the pudding is cooked. Any pudding of the nature of a custard must be very carefully steamed, as extreme heat would curdle the eggs and make the pudding watery.

More solid puddings may be steamed more quickly.

For a steamed pudding three-quarters fill the basin.

A pudding which is to be boiled must be tied over firmly with a cloth which has been wrung out of boiling water and sprinkled with flour.

Have sufficient boiling water in the pan to cover the pudding, and keep it boiling steadily the whole time the pudding is in it.

A kettle of boiling water should be kept at hand to fill up the saucepan when necessary. Fill the basin to the brim for a boiled pudding.

Pudding cloths should be quickly washed after using, and hung in the air to dry.

When suet is used in a pudding, it should be hard and dry.

Remove all skin and fibre from it and shred it as finely as possible.

Dust it over generously with sieved flour, and then chop it finely with a long pointed knife.

Hold down the point of the knife on the board with one hand, and with the other work the handle end up and down.

Any suet, if good, can be used, although beef suet is generally preferred.

Mutton suet, however, makes the lightest puddings, while veal suet is the most delicate.

Currants should be washed in lukewarm water,

rubbed in a cloth to remove the stalks and to dry them. Then drop them a few at a time on a plate or tin to prove by the sound if there are any stones among them or not, and place them in the oven for a few minutes.

Candied peel should have the hard sugar removed from the inside, and then be shred very thinly with a sharp knife.

Sultanas should be rubbed in flour, and have the stalks picked off them.

Use moist sugar for all general sweetening purposes, but castor sugar for all light puddings.

To turn a pudding out of a mould or basin, lift it from the pan, and allow it to stand for a minute or two.

If too great haste is used, the first steam escaping from the pudding will crack it.

Remove the cloth or paper from the top, then take hold of the basin with a cloth and shake it gently to ascertain that it is coming away freely from the sides, then reverse it on a dish, and remove the mould carefully.

When the pudding is in a cloth, untie the strings, and draw the cloth a little from the sides of the pudding; then reverse it on a hot dish, and draw the cloth carefully away.

Notes on Soufflé Making.—This is a class of puddings known only by its French name, and is so generally understood that it has become almost an anglicised word.

A soufflé is a pudding which is made very light by having stiffly beaten whites of eggs added to it or sometimes whipped cream, and of which the basis is a cooked batter, with raw yolks of eggs and some dis-

vii

tinctive flavouring or other ingredient which requires little cooking added to it.

The preparation of a soufflé is exceedingly simple if exact measures are taken, and if the directions given for making it are carefully followed. The only difficulty is in serving it soon enough, as it falls so quickly when taken from the heat. Have everything ready before beginning to make the soufflé. If it is a steamed one, prepare the tin, and put on the saucepan with the water in which it is to be cooked. If, on the other hand, it is a baked soufflé, see that the oven is at a right heat for cooking, and grease the tin or dish to be used.

A soufflé tin is a plain round one with high sides. (A fancy mould is not suitable.) First grease the mould very carefully and thickly with clarified butter. If for a steamed soufflé, cut a double band of paper wide enough to stand three or four inches above the top of the tin and to reach down to the middle of it. Grease this band, and tie it round the outside of the tin, putting the single edges to the top and the double fold below. Also grease a round or square of paper to cover the top.

The whites of eggs for all soufflés must be beaten up very stiffly in a basin with a wire whisk, and folded rather than mixed in to the other ingredients, care being taken not to break them down by too much mixing.

As the mixture rises considerably when cooking, the mould should not be more than half filled. In a steamed soufflé the band of paper forms a protection to prevent the mixture falling over the sides; in a baked soufflé this is not so necessary, as the mixture hardens as it rises.

When steaming a soufflé, cook it very slowly and steadily; the water must only reach half-way up the side of the mould, and merely simmer slowly all the time. If cooked too quickly, the soufflé will rise rapidly without becoming firm, and will then sink in the middle when turned out, and look like a crushed hat. A soufflé is ready when it feels firm to the touch.

Steamed soufflés are always turned out of the moulds in which they are cooked, and a suitable sauce poured round, never over them.

A soufflé that has to be baked should be scored across two or three times on the top to divide the mixture before putting it in the oven, otherwise the first stroke of the spoon when serving it would lift off all the surface skin. The oven for baking them should be moderate and steady.

Baked soufflés are sent to table in the tins in which they are baked, and these are either slipped inside a hot silver case, or a warm serviette is folded round them. China fireproof dishes may be used instead of the tins.

STEAMED OR BOILED PUDDINGS.

Albert Pudding.
Amber Pudding.
Apple Pudding.
Banana Pudding.
Boiled Batter with Fruit.
Bermuda Pudding.
Plain Cabinet Pudding.
Cabinet Pudding with Pineapple.
Coffee Cabinet Pudding.
Casserole of Rice with Stewed Fruit.
Cherry Pudding.
Chester Pudding.
Chestnut and Custard Pudding.
Chocolate Pudding.
Cocoanut Pudding.
Coffee Custards.
Christmas Plum Pudding.
Date Pudding.
Delaware Pudding.
Edith Pudding.
Fig Pudding.
Gâteau of Semolina.
Imperial Pudding.
Jam Roly-Poly.
Lemon Pudding.
Little Doris Puddings.
Little Russian Puddings.
Orange Pudding.
Preserved Ginger Pudding.
Prune Pudding.
Raspberry Pudding.

x

Redcap Pudding.
Rice and Orange-Marmalade Pudding.
Snowdon Pudding.
Suet Pastry.
Sultana Pudding.
Treacle Sponge.
Walnut Pudding.
Winchester Puddings.

1.—ALBERT PUDDING.

Ingredients—

3 Eggs.	4 oz. Butter.
6 oz. Flour.	Grated rind of 1 Lemon.
6 oz. Castor Sugar.	1 oz. Valencia Raisins.

Method—

First cut the raisins in halves, stone them, and dry them for a few minutes on a plate in the oven. Then grease a mould, and decorate it with the prepared raisins.

To Make the Mixture.—Sieve the sugar into a basin, add the butter, and beat these two together with a wooden spoon until of a creamy consistency. Then add the eggs, one at a time, along with a little flour sieved, beating well between each. Flavour with grated lemon rind or any other flavouring preferred, and pour the mixture into the prepared mould. Cover with greased paper, and steam from one and a half to two hours. Turn out carefully and serve with Jam or Custard Sauce (see Recipes 118 or 116).

2.—AMBER PUDDING.

Ingredients—

6 oz. Bread-crumbs.
4 oz. minced Apple.
2 oz. Sugar.
2 oz. Flour.
4 oz. chopped Suet.
1 teaspoonful Baking Powder.

2 tablespoonfuls Golden Syrup.
2 Eggs.
A pinch of Nutmeg.
A pinch of Salt.
A little grated Lemon Rind.

Method—

Mix all the dry ingredients together in a basin, and make a well in the centre. Add the syrup slightly warmed, and the two eggs well beaten, and mix together, adding a little milk if necessary. Pour the mixture into a well-greased mould or basin, and cover with a scalded and floured cloth. Plunge the pudding into a saucepan of boiling water, and boil quickly for two hours, keeping the basin well covered all the time. Then turn out, and serve with Lemon or Orange Sauce, (see Recipes 119 or 120).

3.—APPLE PUDDING.

Ingredients—

Suet Crust (Recipe 35).
1 lb. Apples.
2 tablespoonfuls cold Water.

$\frac{1}{4}$ lb. Sugar.
A little grated Lemon Rind or 2 or 3 Cloves.

Method—

Wipe the apples with a damp cloth and peel them thinly. Then cut them in quarters, remove the cores, and slice them thinly. Roll out the pastry to about quarter of an inch in thickness, grease a basin, and

line it with it.   Press the pastry well on to the sides
of the basin, and try to keep it of a uniform thickness.
Cut off the trimmings, and roll them out in a round
shape, large enough to cover the pudding.   Fill up
the basin with the apples, sugar, and flavouring, pressing them well down, as the fruit sinks considerably
when cooking.   Wet the edge of the pastry which
lines the basin, put on the cover, and press the two
edges well together.   Dip the centre of a pudding-
cloth in boiling water, and dredge it with flour.   Tie
this over the top of the pudding, and plunge it into a
saucepan of fast boiling water.   Boil quickly for two
hours at least.   More boiling water must be added as
required.   When ready, turn out on a hot dish, and
serve at once.

NOTES.—Any other fruit may be used instead of
apples, and the amount of sugar will vary according to
the acidity of the fruit.   Gooseberries must be topped
and tailed and washed in cold water; plums washed
in cold water, and if time permits, stoned; rhubarb
wiped and cut in small pieces.   All fruit must be carefully prepared before being put in.

4.—BANANA PUDDING.

Ingredients—

½ pint Milk.
3 yolks of Eggs.
2 whites of Eggs.
1 tablespoonful Cake-
    crumbs.

1 dessertspoonful Sugar.
A few drops of Vanilla.
4 or 5 Bananas.
The juice of ½ Lemon.
1 tablespoonful Sugar.

½ glass Sherry or Rum.

Method—

Peel the bananas, removing all pith and string, and
slice them lengthways with a silver knife.   Put them

on to a plate, sprinkle them with the sugar, lemon juice, and wine, and let them soak for half hour, turning the pieces occasionally. Meanwhile, make a custard. Beat up the yolks and whites of eggs in a basin with one dessertspoonful of sugar and a few drops of vanilla or any other flavouring. Heat the milk almost to boiling point, and pour it on to the eggs, &c., stirring all the time. Then strain the custard into another basin, add the cake-crumbs, and allow it to cool.

Grease a plain tin mould, and arrange the bananas in it crosswise; pour the custard slowly over them, and cover with greased paper. Place this pudding in a steamer, and steam very slowly for at least one hour, or until it feels firm to the touch. Or it may be cooked in a saucepan with hot water to reach half-way up the sides of the mould, but in this case a double fold of paper should be placed below the mould, to prevent the top of the pudding cooking too quickly and becoming tough.

This pudding may be served either hot or cold, and a jam or custard sauce, to which any liquid left from the bananas should be added, may be poured round it.

5.—BOILED BATTER WITH FRUIT.

Ingredients—

¼ lb. Flour.	2 teaspoonfuls Baking
½ pint Milk.	Powder.
Fruit.	2 Eggs.

A pinch of Salt.

Method—

Sieve the flour into a basin with the salt and the baking powder. Make a well in the centre, and add the two eggs without beating them. Mix the flour gradually into these, and then add the milk by degrees. Beat the batter well, and then add as much fruit as it will hold. Apples, cherries, raspberries, or straw-berries are about the best fruits to use. Apples would require to be peeled, cored, and sliced, cherries stoned, and raspberries or strawberries carefully picked. Pour the mixture into a well-greased mould, and tie a scalded and floured cloth over the top. Plunge the pudding into a saucepan of boiling water, and boil quickly for one hour. Serve with fruit syrup or any nice sweet sauce.

6.—BERMUDA PUDDING.

Ingredients—

2 Eggs.	½ teaspoonful Baking
¼ lb. Flour.	Powder.
¼ lb. Castor Sugar.	1½ tablespoonfuls
2 oz. Butter.	Orange Marmalade.

Method—

Sieve the sugar into a basin, add the butter, and beat these two together with a wooden spoon until of a creamy consistency. If the butter is very hard, stand the basin for a minute or two in the oven or over a saucepan of hot water. Add one egg and half the flour sieved, and beat for a few minutes, then the second egg and the rest of the flour. Mix well, and add the baking powder and marmalade at the last. Pour into a well-greased mould, cover with greased paper, and steam gently for one and a half hours. Serve with Wine Sauce (Recipe 126) or a little melted marmalade round the base.

7.—PLAIN CABINET PUDDING.

Ingredients—

2 slices of Bread and Butter.	2 oz. Valencia Raisins.
1 oz. Sugar.	2 Eggs.
	½ pint Milk.

A little Flavouring.

Method—

Cut the bread rather less than half an inch in thickness, remove the crusts, and butter it. Then cut it in pieces about one inch square. Stone the raisins, cut them in halves, and put them on a plate in the oven for two or three minutes to dry. Grease thoroughly a plain mould or basin, and decorate it with some of the raisins. Lay in the bread very loosely with the sugar and the rest of the raisins. Beat up the eggs in another basin, add the milk and flavouring to them, and then strain over the bread. Cover the pudding with a piece of greased paper, and let it stand for half an hour so as to thoroughly soak the bread. Then steam very slowly about one hour, or until the pudding feels firm to the touch. Let the pudding stand for a minute or two after removing it from the pan to allow some of the steam to escape, then turn out carefully on to a hot dish. Serve with Custard or Jam Sauce (Recipes 116 or 118).

8.—CABINET PUDDING WITH PINEAPPLE.

Ingredients—

3 or 4 slices of Bread.	½ pint Milk.
½ lb. tinned Pineapple.	2 Eggs.
	1 tablespoonful Sugar.

Method—

Grease a plain round mould, and cut the bread in
rounds to fit it.   Drain the pineapple, and cut it into
small pieces.   Fill the mould with alternate layers of
bread and pineapple.   Beat up the eggs with the
sugar, and add the milk.   Strain this custard into
the mould, cover with greased paper, and allow the
pudding to stand for half an hour before cooking, so
that the bread may become thoroughly soaked.   Then
place the mould in a tin with hot water to come half-
way up the sides, and cook in a slow oven from a
half to three-quarters of an hour, or until the custard
is set.   Let it stand in the mould for a few minutes
after it is cooked.   When ready to serve, turn carefully
out, and serve with Pineapple Sauce (see Recipe 121).

NOTE.—Sponge-cake cut in slices may be used in
place of bread, and a little liqueur added for flavouring
is an improvement.

9.—COFFEE CABINET PUDDING.

Ingredients—

5 oz. Bread.	1 oz. Butter.
1 gill strong black Coffee.	3 Eggs.
	1 oz. Sugar.

1 oz. Sweet Almonds.

Method—

Weigh the bread free from crust, put it into a basin,
pour the coffee over, and let it soak for half an hour.
In another basin melt the butter, and add the sugar,
yolks of eggs, and almonds blanched and chopped.
Mix these well together until of a creamy consistency,
squeeze the bread out lightly, and beat it into the rest
of the ingredients.   Then whisk the whites of the

eggs to a stiff froth, and stir them in very lightly at the last. Pour the mixture into a well-greased mould, cover with greased paper, and steam slowly for one and a half hours. Serve with Custard Sauce made with equal quantities of coffee and milk (see Recipe 116).

10.—CASSEROLE OF RICE WITH STEWED FRUIT.

Ingredients—

$\frac{1}{4}$ lb. Carolina Rice.	Rind of $\frac{1}{2}$ Lemon.
1 gill of Water.	2 oz. Sugar.
1 pint Milk.	Stewed Apples or
2 Eggs.	Prunes.

Method—

Wash the rice well in several waters, and then put it into a lined saucepan with one gill of fresh cold water. Bring to the boil, and cook for two or three minutes. Then add the milk and the rind of half a lemon peeled off very thinly. Simmer slowly from half to three-quarters of an hour until the rice is quite soft and has absorbed all the milk. Stir occasionally whilst it is cooking to prevent it sticking to the pan. When ready, remove the pan from the fire, and add the sugar and the two eggs well beaten. Mix well, and remove the lemon rind. Pour the mixture into a greased border mould, cover with greased paper, and steam slowly for half an hour or until firm to the touch. Then lift the pudding from the pan, and allow it to stand for a few minutes. Turn out very carefully on a hot dish, and fill the centre with stewed apples, prunes, or any other suitable fruit, pouring some of the syrup from the fruit round the base.

11.—CHERRY PUDDING.

Ingredients—

½ lb. fresh Cherries.
2½ oz. brown Bread-
    Crumbs.
Grated rind of ½ Lemon.
1½ oz. Castor Sugar.

1 gill Milk or Cream.
2 Eggs.
1 oz. Loaf Sugar.
The juice of ½ Lemon.
¾ gill of Water.

Method—

Put the bread-crumbs, sugar, and grated lemon rind into a basin. Wash, pick, and stone the cherries, and add three-quarters of them to the bread-crumbs, &c. Boil the milk or cream, and pour it over the crumbs and fruit. Add the yolks of eggs, and lastly the whites beaten to a stiff froth. Pour the mixture into a well-greased mould or basin, and cover with buttered paper. Place the pudding in a saucepan with enough boiling water to come half-way up the sides of the mould, put on the lid, and steam slowly and steadily for one hour. Make a sauce with the remainder of the cherries, water, lemon juice, and loaf sugar. Put all these ingredients into a saucepan, and boil gently from ten to fifteen minutes. Add two or three drops of carmine to make it a pretty pink colour.

Turn the pudding carefully on to a hot dish, and pour the sauce round it.

12.—CHESTER PUDDING.

Ingredients—

1 teacupful Flour.
1 teacupful Sugar.
1 teacupful Bread-
    Crumbs.
1 teacupful chopped
    Suet.

1 teacupful Milk.
1 teacupful Black-
    currant Jam.
½ teaspoonful Carbo-
    nate of Soda.
A pinch of Salt.

Method—

Chop the suet finely, and put it into a basin with the bread-crumbs, flour, sugar, and salt. Mix these dry ingredients together, make a well in the centre, and put in the jam. Heat the milk slightly in a small saucepan, add the soda, free from lumps, and mix quickly. Pour this while still frothy on to the top of the jam, and mix all together. Put the mixture into a greased mould or basin, cover with a scalded and floured cloth, and boil for three hours. Serve with Jam Sauce (Recipe 118).

13.—CHESTNUT AND CUSTARD PUDDING.

Ingredients—

24 Chestnuts.	½ pint Milk.
1 gill Water.	3 yolks of Eggs.
2 oz. Sugar.	2 whites of Eggs.
Rind of ½ Lemon.	1 oz. Sugar.

CARAMEL.

3 oz. Loaf Sugar.	A squeeze of Lemon
½ gill Water.	Juice.

Method—

To peel the chestnuts, cut them round lightly with a knife; put them into a stewpan with sufficient cold water to cover them, and boil them for five minutes, Then drain them, and peel off both the shell and the inner skin. Put the chestnuts thus prepared into a saucepan with the water, lemon rind, and sugar, and stew them until soft and nearly dry. Then rub them through a wire sieve.

Make the Caramel according to directions given in Recipe 22, and line a plain mould with it.

Make a custard with the eggs, sugar, and milk. Beat up the yolks and whites of eggs in a basin with the sugar. Heat the milk almost to boiling point, and pour it over them, stirring all the time ; then strain, and allow it to cool. Add the chestnut purée to the custard, and fill up the mould which has been lined with the caramel. Cover with greased paper, and steam very slowly for one and a half hours, or until firm to the touch. Serve with Wine Sauce (see Recipe 127).

14.—CHOCOLATE PUDDING.

Ingredients—

2 or 3 oz. Chocolate.	1 gill of Milk.
5 oz. Bread-crumbs.	2 Eggs.
3 oz. Butter.	A few drops of Vanilla.
3 oz. Castor Sugar.	A pinch of Cinnamon.

Method—

Cut the chocolate into small pieces, and dissolve it slowly in the milk. Cream the butter and sugar together in a basin, add the yolks of eggs and a few of the bread-crumbs, and mix well ; then the dissolved chocolate, vanilla, and the rest of the crumbs, and mix again. Whip the whites of eggs to a stiff froth, and mix them in lightly at the last. Pour the mixture into a well-greased mould, and steam slowly for one and a half hours, until the pudding is well risen, and feels firm to the touch. Serve with Chocolate, Custard, or Wine Sauce (see Recipes 115, 116, 127).

15.—COCOANUT PUDDING.

Ingredients—

2 oz. Bread-crumbs.	3 gills Milk.
2 oz. Cake-crumbs.	3 Eggs.
2 oz. Butter.	A few drops of Vanilla.
2 oz. Castor Sugar.	3 oz. Cocoanut.

Method—

Put the cocoanut into a saucepan with the milk, and cook slowly over the fire from ten to fifteen minutes. Sieve the sugar into a basin, add the butter, and beat these two together with a wooden spoon until of a creamy consistency; then add the yolks of eggs, flavouring, cocoanut, &c., and mix well together. Beat the whites of eggs to a stiff froth, and mix them in lightly at the last. Pour the mixture into a well-greased mould, cover with greased paper, and steam slowly for one and a half hours. When firm to the touch, turn carefully out, and, serve with Wine or Custard Sauce (see Recipes 126, 116).

16.—COFFEE CUSTARDS.

Ingredients—

4 yolks of Eggs.	1 gill strong clear
2 whites of Eggs.	Coffee.
1 gill Milk or Cream.	1 oz. Sugar.

Method—

Beat up the yolks and whites of eggs in a basin with the sugar, add the coffee and milk or cream, and mix well together. A few drops of liqueur may also be added. Strain the custard, and pour it into small greased cups or basins. Place them in a stewpan sufficiently large to hold them, and put in boiling water, which must only reach half-way up the cups. Cover over with a round of white paper greased, and put the lid on the pan. Simmer very slowly until the custards are set, about fifteen minutes, then allow them to stand for a minute or two before turning them out. Serve with whipped Wine Sauce (see Recipe 126).

17.—CHRISTMAS PLUM PUDDING.

Ingredients—

2 lbs. Valencia Raisins.	2 Bitter Almonds.
2 lbs. Currants.	1 tablespoonful Mixed
2 lbs. Sultanas.	Spice.
2½ lbs. Sugar.	½ teaspoonful Salt.
2 lbs. Suet.	Rind and juice of 3
1 lb. Flour.	Lemons.
½ lb. Apples.	1 glass of Brandy.
1½ lb. Bread-crumbs.	1 glass of Rum.
½ lb. mixed Peel.	12 Eggs.
½ lb. Sweet Almonds.	Milk if necessary.

Method—

First prepare the fruit. Stone the raisins and chop them slightly. Pick and clean the currants and sultanas. Shred the peel and blanch and chop the almonds. Peel and chop the apples, and grate the rind very thinly from the lemons. Put all the fruit into a large basin or crock, add the other dry ingredients and mix thoroughly. Then beat the eggs, and add them with the wine, lemon juice, and enough milk to bind all together. Mix again with a long spoon, cover the mixture, and let it stand for twenty-four hours before

cooking. Then fill up moulds or basins with the
mixture, tie over them a scalded and floured cloth,
and boil from six to eight hours according to size.
Keep the puddings in a cool place for several weeks
before using them, and reboil for several hours as
required. Before serving the pudding, pour a wine-
glassful of brandy round the base, and set a light to it
just before putting it on the table. The dish must be
hot and perfectly dry, or the brandy will not burn well.

NOTES.—A little grated orange rind and juice may
be added to the above mixture.

Remains of cold plum pudding are very good cut
in slices and fried.

18.—DATE PUDDING.

Ingredients—

¼ lb. Dates.	½ teaspoonful Mixed
2 oz. Sugar.	Spice.
3 oz. Suet.	¼ teaspoonful Baking
2 oz. Bread-crumbs.	Powder.
2 oz. Flour.	A little Milk.
1 Egg.	A pinch of Salt.

1 tablespoonful Treacle.

Method—

Stone the dates and cut them in small pieces.
Remove all skin from the suet, shred it finely, and
then weigh it. Chop it finely with a knife, sprinkling
it with the flour to prevent it from sticking to the
board. Then mix all the dry ingredients together in a
basin, and make a well in the centre. Add the eggs
well beaten, the treacle slightly warmed, and enough
milk to make all of a softish consistency. Pour the

mixture into a well-greased mould, cover with a lid
or with greased paper, and steam steadily for at least
two hours. Turn out on a hot dish, and serve with
Lemon or any other suitable sauce.

19.—DELAWARE PUDDING.

Ingredients—

Suet Crust.
1 or 2 Apples.
1 oz. Currants.
1 oz. Candied Peel.
$\frac{1}{2}$ Lemon.
1 oz. Butter.
1 teaspoonful Mixed Spice.
2 oz. Demerara Sugar.

Method—

First prepare the mixture. Peel, core, and chop
the apples finely. Clean the currants and shred the
peel. Mix all these together in a basin with the
spice. Put the sugar and butter on to a plate, grate
the lemon rind over, and work them well together with
a knife. Then add them to the other ingredients in
the basin, strain the lemon juice over, and mix again.

Grease a pint basin, and make some suet crust
according to Recipe 35. Roll out the pastry
rather thinly, and cut it out in rounds to fit the basin
with a cutter or saucepan lid. Put first a round of
pastry into the basin, then a spoonful of the mixture,
another round of pastry, and so on until the basin is
full. Make the last layer pastry, covering well over.
Cover the basin with a scalded and floured cloth, and
tie it firmly on. Plunge the pudding into a saucepan
of fast boiling water, and boil quickly for at least two
hours. When ready, turn out carefully on to a hot
dish. and serve with or without sauce.

NOTE.—Treacle, syrup, or jam may be used instead of the mixture. Treacle or syrup should first be mixed with bread-crumbs or oatmeal to thicken it, and nicely flavoured with lemon or ginger.

20.—EDITH PUDDING.

Ingredients—

1 oz. fine Tapioca.	2 tablespoonfuls Jam.
½ pint Milk.	2 Eggs.
1 oz. Sugar.	Rind and juice of ½
2 oz. Butter.	Lemon.

4 penny Sponge-cakes.

Method—

Grease a pudding mould, and dust it out with cake-crumbs. Then put into a saucepan the milk, tapioca, and butter, and stir these over the fire until boiling. Cook for two or three minutes until the tapioca swells and thickens, then remove the pan from the fire. Add the sugar, the grated lemon rind, and the two eggs well beaten, and mix all together. Slice the sponge-cakes, spread them with jam, and cut in dice. Then put them into the prepared mould, squeeze the lemon juice over, and fill up with the tapioca mixture. Cover with greased paper, and steam this pudding slowly for two hours. Serve with Wine or Jam Sauce (see Recipes 126 or 118).

NOTE.—The sponge-cakes may be soaked in wine or liqueur if wished, and a little cream may be added to the mixture.

21.—FIG PUDDING.

Ingredients—

½ lb. Figs.	1 teaspoonful Mixed
6 oz. Suet.	Spices.
¼ lb. Bread-crumbs.	A pinch of Salt.
¼ lb. Flour.	½ teaspoonful Baking
¼ lb. Sugar.	Powder.
2 Eggs.	½ pint Milk.

Method—

Soak the figs in boiling water for ten minutes, then dry them and cut them in small pieces, removing the stalks. Sieve the flour into a basin, add the suet finely chopped, the sugar, bread-crumbs, spices, baking powder, and salt, and mix all lightly together with the fingers. Then add the figs, mix again, and make a well in the centre. Beat the eggs in another basin, and pour them into the centre of the dry ingredients. Add also the milk, and stir well together. Pour the mixture into a greased mould or basin, cover with a lid or piece of greased paper, and steam steadily for at least four hours. Serve with Custard or Wine Sauce (see Recipes 116 or 126).

Notes.—This pudding may be made richer by adding two ounces of candied peel and two ounces of sweet almonds. A little wine may also be added and less milk.

22.—GÂTEAU OF SEMOLINA.

Ingredients—

2 oz. Semolina.	1 pint Milk.
1 oz. Sugar.	2 Eggs.

Flavouring.

CARAMEL.

2 oz. Loaf Sugar.	A squeeze of Lemon
½ gill Water.	Juice.

Method—

Rinse out a small saucepan with cold water, and put into it the semolina and the milk. Stir these over the fire until boiling, then simmer from ten to fifteen minutes until the semolina is quite cooked and the mixture thick. Remove the pan from the fire, and add the sugar flavouring to taste, and the two eggs well beaten. Mix well. To make the caramel, put the sugar, water, and lemon juice into a small iron saucepan or sugar-boiler, and let them boil until they become a golden brown colour. Watch it carefully, as it quickly browns. Then pour the caramel into a plain mould, one and a half pint size ; take hold of the mould with a cloth, as it will be very hot, and run the caramel over the bottom and sides, coating them well. Allow this to cool for a few minutes, then pour in the semolina mixture, and cover over with greased paper. Steam slowly for three-quarters of an hour, or bake in a moderate oven for half hour. This may be served either hot or cold. Turn out carefully when wanted.

23.—IMPERIAL PUDDING.

Ingredients—

¾ lb. Prunes.	Juice of ½ Lemon.
¼ lb. Honey or Syrup.	Brown Sugar.

SUET CRUST.

¾ lb. Flour.	A pinch of Salt.
6 oz. Suet.	Cold Water.

Method—

Well grease a plain mould or basin, and coat the inside with coarse brown sugar. Then wash the prunes, and let them soak in boiling water for half an hour. Meanwhile make the suet crust according to Recipe 35, and roll it out rather thinly. Cut a round from this, and lay it at the foot of the basin. Put a layer of prunes, stoned, on the top, and squeeze over a little lemon juice. Then place over another round of pastry with some honey on the top, more pastry, more prunes, and so on, until the basin is full. The last layer should be of the pastry. Cover with a scalded and floured cloth, plunge into boiling water, and boil at least three hours. Serve with Lemon Sauce (Recipe 119).

NOTE.—Dates may be used instead of prunes, and syrup or any nice jam instead of the honey.

24.—JAM ROLY-POLY.

Ingredients—

3 or 4 tablespoonfuls of Jam.   Suet Pastry.

Method—

Make some suet crust according to Recipe 35, and roll it out into an oblong shape about quarter inch in thickness. Keep it as even at the edges as possible, and do not let it stick to the board. Wet round the edges of the pastry with cold water, and then spread with jam. Keep the jam about an inch from the edge all round. Roll up in the form of a bolster, sealing the edges well together. Dip a pudding cloth in boiling water, and dredge it with flour. Wrap up the pudding in this, leaving room for it to swell, and tie firmly at both ends. Plunge the pudding into a saucepan of fast boiling water, with a plate at the foot, and boil at least two hours. When ready, lift out, and let it stand for a minute or two. Then undo the cloth carefully, and turn out the pudding on to a hot dish. Wipe any water off the dish, and serve hot.

NOTES.—If the jam is very liquid, a few bread-crumbs or a little oatmeal should be mixed with it. Treacle or syrup may be used instead of jam, or some-times mince-meat or raw sugar.

25.—LEMON PUDDING.

Make in the same way as Orange Pudding (Recipe 28), substituting lemon for the orange, and using rather a smaller quantity of rind.

26.—LITTLE DORIS PUDDINGS.

Ingredients—

2 oz. Bread-crumbs.	2 oz. Sugar.
2 oz. Flour.	1 gill of Milk.
2 oz. Suet.	½ teaspoonful Baking
2 oz. Chocolate Powder.	Powder.

A few glacé Cherries.

Method—

Grease well seven or eight small moulds or tiny basins, and decorate them at the foot with small pieces of glacé cherry. Chop the suet finely, and put it into a basin with the flour, bread-crumbs, sugar, and baking powder. Mix these dry ingredients well together. Then put the chocolate into a small saucepan with the milk, and simmer over the fire for a few minutes until quite dissolved and smooth. Pour this into the basin, and mix all together, adding a little more milk if necessary. Three-quarters fill the prepared moulds, stand them in a saucepan with boiling water to come half-way up the sides, and cover with greased paper. Put the lid on the pan, and steam the puddings steadily for one hour, until well risen, and firm to the touch. Turn out, and serve with Custard or Chocolate Sauce (see Recipes 116 or 115).

NOTE.—This pudding may be made richer by adding one egg well beaten to the mixture.

27.—LITTLE RUSSIAN PUDDINGS.

Ingredients—

2 Eggs, their weight in Butter, Flour, and Castor Sugar.

½ teaspoonful Baking Powder.

2 or 3 drops of Vanilla.

2 or 3 drops of Essence of Lemon.

1 dessert-spoonful grated Chocolate.

2 or 3 drops of Carmine.

Method—

Sieve the sugar into a basin, add the butter, and beat these two together with a wooden spoon until of a creamy consistency. Then add one egg with a little of the flour sieved and beat well, then another egg with a little more flour, beat again, and repeat this until all the eggs and flour are incorporated. When the mixture looks light and shows air-bubbles, add the baking powder, and then divide it into three equal portions. To one portion add the chocolate, to another a few drops of carmine to make it a pretty pink colour and two or three drops of essence of almonds to flavour, and leave the third portion its natural colour, flavouring with vanilla. Have about nine small moulds or dariols well greased, and put into them alternate spoonfuls of the different mixtures. Fill them rather irregularly, and then shake the mixture down. They should not be more than three-quarters full. Put them into a saucepan with a double fold of paper at the foot, pour in enough hot water to come half-way up the sides, and cover with greased paper. Put the lid on the pan, and steam the puddings slowly for half an hour. Then turn them out and serve with Custard Sauce (Recipe 116).

28.—ORANGE PUDDING.

Ingredients—

¼ lb. Bread-crumbs.	The grated rind of 2
2 oz. Flour.	Oranges and the juice
2 oz. Rice Flour.	of 1.
3 oz. Castor Sugar.	¼ lb. chopped Suet.
¼ teaspoonful Baking	A little Milk.
Powder.	A pinch of Salt.

Method—

Wipe the oranges with a damp cloth, and grate the rind off them on to the top of the sugar. Work the sugar and orange rind together with a broad-bladed knife until they are thoroughly blended. Then chop the suet finely, using some of the flour to prevent it sticking to the board and knife. Mix all the dry ingredients together in a basin, and make a well in the centre. Add the orange juice strained, the eggs well beaten, and enough milk to make all of a softish consistency. Pour the mixture into a greased mould

or basin, cover with a lid or with greased paper, and
steam or boil for at least two hours. Serve with
Orange Sauce (Recipe 120).

29.—PRESERVED GINGER PUDDING.

Ingredients—

2 Eggs.	1 tablespoonful Ginger
3 oz. Butter.	Syrup.
3 oz. Castor Sugar.	$\frac{1}{4}$ teaspoonful Baking
2 oz. Flour.	Powder.
2 oz. Rice Flour.	$\frac{1}{4}$ teaspoonful ground
$\frac{1}{4}$ lb. preserved Ginger.	Ginger.

Method—

Put the butter into a basin, and sieve the sugar on
the top of it. Beat these two together with a wooden
spoon until of a creamy consistency. Then add the
eggs and the two flours by degrees. Beat well for a
few minutes. Cut the ginger into small pieces, and
mix it in lightly at the last with the baking powder,
ginger syrup, and ground ginger. Pour the mixture
into a well-greased mould, cover with greased paper,
and steam slowly for one and a half hours. Turn out
on a hot dish, and pour Custard Sauce (Recipe 116)
round.

30.—PRUNE PUDDING.

Ingredients—

$\frac{1}{2}$ lb. Prunes.	$1\frac{1}{2}$ oz. Sweet Almonds.
2 oz. Sugar.	$\frac{1}{2}$ pint Milk.
$\frac{1}{2}$ pint Water.	2 tablespoonfuls Port
3 Eggs.	or Claret.
$\frac{1}{4}$ lb. Ratafia or Maca-	A few drops of Car-
roon Crumbs.	mine.

Methods—

Wash the prunes, and allow them to soak for one hour in the half pint of water. Then turn them into a saucepan with the water, and add the sugar. Simmer until quite soft, then strain (reserving the liquor), and remove the stones from the prunes. Grease a plain mould very carefully, and coat the sides with macaroon or ratafia crumbs. Arrange a layer of the cooked prunes at the foot of the mould, sprinkle with some of the almonds blanched and chopped, and then put in a layer of crumbs, then more prunes, &c.; and repeat this until all the crumbs and prunes are used. Beat up the eggs, add the milk, and strain this custard into the mould. (The mould should not be more than three-quarters full.) Cover with greased paper, and steam very slowly for three-quarters of an hour, or until firm to the touch. Reheat the liquid from the prunes, reducing it a little if necessary, and add to it the wine and a few drops of carmine. Turn the pudding carefully out, and pour this sauce round.

31.—RASPBERRY PUDDING.

Ingredients—

4 oz. Suet.	1 teacupful Raspberry
4 oz. Flour.	Purée.
2 oz. Brown Sugar.	1 teaspoonful Carbo-
1 or 2 Eggs.	nate of Soda.
2 or 3 drops of Carmine.	1 gill of Milk.

Method—

Prepare the purée of raspberries by rubbing either fresh or bottled raspberries through a hair sieve.

Chop the suet very finely, and mix it in a basin with
the flour and sugar. Make a well in the centre, and
add the purée, a few drops of carmine, and the egg or
eggs well beaten. Heat the milk slightly, and stir the
soda into it. Add this to the other ingredients, and
mix all together. Pour into a well-greased mould,
cover with greased paper, and steam for two and a
half hours. Serve with a cold purée of raspberries or
whipped cream.

32.—REDCAP PUDDING.

Ingredients—

2 or 3 oz. Glacé Cherries.	¼ lb. Sugar.
¼ lb. Suet.	¼ lb. Bread-crumbs.
	2 small Eggs.

Juice of 1 Lemon.

Method—

First make the bread-crumbs by rubbing some
rather stale bread through a wire sieve. Then chop
the suet finely, sprinkling it with some of the crumbs
to prevent it sticking to the board and knife. Mix
together the bread-crumbs, suet, and sugar, and
moisten with the eggs well beaten and the lemon
juice strained. Grease a plain mould or basin,
decorate the top of it with the cherries cut in halves,
and then fill up with the mixture. Cover with greased
paper, and steam at least two hours. Turn out, and
serve with Lemon Sauce (Recipe 119).

33.—RICE AND ORANGE-MARMALADE PUDDING.

Ingredients—

¼ lb. Rice.	1 oz. Butter.
½ pint Water.	3 Eggs.
1 quart Milk.	2 tablespoonfuls
4 oz. Sugar.	Marmalade.

A pinch of Salt.

Method—

Wash the rice in several waters until quite clean, and then put it into a lined saucepan with half pint fresh cold water. Bring to the boil, and pour the water off. Add the milk and butter, and simmer slowly until the rice is quite soft and thick. Stir well from time to time, or cook in a double saucepan. When ready, add the yolks of eggs and half the sugar. Pour the mixture into a greased pie-dish, and bake about fifteen minutes in a moderate oven. Then spread the top of the pudding rather thickly with marmalade. Add a pinch of salt to the whites of eggs, and beat them up to a stiff froth. Sieve the remainder of the sugar over them, and pile this meringue over the marmalade. Return the pudding to a moderate oven until the meringue is nicely browned and set, and sprinkle with sugar before serving.

34.—SNOWDON PUDDING.

Ingredients—

4 oz. Suet.	2 tablespoonfuls Marmalade.
4 oz. Ground Rice.	
4 oz. Bread-crumbs.	A pinch of Salt.
4 oz. Brown Sugar.	A few Raisins.
A little Milk.	1 Egg.

Method—

Cut the raisins in halves, stone them, and dry them for a few minutes on a plate in the oven. Then grease a mould or basin, and decorate it with the prepared raisins.

To Make the Pudding.—First chop the suet finely, and put it into a basin with the bread-crumbs, ground rice, sugar, and salt. Mix these dry ingredients together, and then make a well in the centre. Add the marmalade, the egg well beaten, and enough milk to moisten. Mix well, and pour into the prepared mould. Cover with greased paper, and steam for three hours. Serve with Custard or Wine Sauce (see Recipes 116 or 126).

NOTE.—The milk may be omitted and wine or brandy added.

35.—SUET PASTRY.

Proportions—

½ lb. Flour.	¼ teaspoonful Baking
¼ lb. Suet.	Powder.
½ teaspoonful Salt.	Cold Water.

Method—

Weigh the flour carefully, add the salt and baking powder to it, and rub these through a wire sieve into a clean dry basin. Remove the skin from the suet, shred it very finely with a sharp knife, and then weigh it. Put it on to a chopping board, and sprinkle it with some of the flour already weighed out. Then chop it very finely, using enough flour to prevent it sticking to the board and knife. The finer it is chopped, the better the pastry will be. When ready, mix it thoroughly with the flour in the basin, rubbing all the ingredients

lightly together with the tips of the fingers. Then
make a well in the centre of these dry ingredients, and
add cold water very gradually with the left hand while
you mix with the right. Mix with the hand or with a
knife. Form into a smooth soft dough, and turn out
on to a floured board, leaving the basin quite clean.
Work lightly with the hands until free from cracks,
then flour a rolling pin and roll out to the thickness
required. Roll on the one side only, and be careful
the pastry does not stick to the board nor roller. Lift
it gently at the sides from time to time to make sure of
this, and dust a little flour under and over as required.
Use no more flour than is necessary for this purpose,
as too much will make the pastry hard.

NOTE.—Buttermilk or sweet milk may be used
instead of water for mixing.

Half the quantity of flour may be omitted, and
¼ lb. bread-crumbs used in its place.

36.—SULTANA PUDDING.

Ingredients—

1 lb. Flour.	1 teaspoonful Baking
6 oz. Suet.	Powder.
6 oz. Sultanas.	Milk.

Method—

Sieve the flour into a clean dry basin. Shred and
chop the suet finely, using a little of the flour to
prevent it from sticking to the board and knife.
Clean and pick the sultanas, and mix all the dry
ingredients together. Then moisten with sufficient
milk to make a stiffish dough. Roll the mixture into
the shape of a bolster, and tie it up like a roly-poly in

a scalded and floured cloth. Plunge the pudding
into a saucepan of boiling water with a plate at the
foot, and boil quickly for at least three hours. Turn
out, and serve hot, accompanied by Lemon or Orange
Sauce.

37.—TREACLE SPONGE.

Ingredients—

½ lb. Flour.
6 oz. Suet.
½ teaspoonful ground
 Cinnamon.
1 teaspoonful ground
 Ginger.

½ teaspoonful Carbo-
 nate of Soda.
¾ cup of Milk.
¼ cup of Treacle.
1 Egg.
A pinch of Salt.

Method—

Sieve the flour into a basin to free it from any
lumps. Remove all skin from the suet, shred it very
finely with a knife, and then weigh it. Chop it very
finely with a knife, using some of the flour already
weighed out to prevent it from sticking to the board.
Then mix with the flour, adding the ginger, cinnamon,
and salt. Mix all lightly together with the fingers
until free from lumps, and then make a well in the
centre. Add the treacle slightly warmed and the egg
well beaten. Heat the milk in a small saucepan, and
add the soda to it. Then mix all together for a few
minutes, and pour the mixture into a well-greased
mould or basin, leaving room for the pudding to rise.
Cover with greased paper, and steam from two to
three hours. When ready, the pudding should be
well risen and feel firm to the touch. Turn out
carefully and serve with Custard Sauce.

38.—WALNUT PUDDING.

Ingredients—

¼ lb. shelled Walnuts.	2 tablespoonfuls Milk.
3 Eggs.	A few drops of Vanilla.
3 oz. Butter.	1 dessertspoonful
3 oz. Castor Sugar.	grated Chocolate.
2 oz. Flour.	½ teaspoonful Baking
2 oz. Rice Flour.	Powder.

Method—

Toast the walnuts in the oven for a few minutes, and then chop them finely or pound them in a mortar. Cream the butter and sugar together in a basin, add the walnuts, and then the eggs and flour by degrees. Beat the mixture well between each egg that is added. Melt the chocolate in the milk, and add it with the baking powder and flavouring. Grease a pudding mould, and decorate it nicely with a few pieces of angelica and glacé cherries. Pour the mixture into it, cover with greased paper, and steam slowly for one and a half hours. Turn out and serve with Custard or Chocolate Sauce (see Sauces 116, 115).

39.—WINCHESTER PUDDINGS.

Ingredients—

4 oz. Flour.	½ teaspoonful Mixed
4 oz. Suet.	Spice.
4 oz. Bread-crumbs.	½ teaspoonful Carbo-
4 oz. Currants.	nate of Soda.
A pinch of Salt.	About 1 teacupful of
4 oz. Raisins.	Milk.
4 oz. Sugar.	

Method—

Chop the suet very finely, using a little of the flour. Clean the currants, and stone and chop the raisins. Mix all the dry ingredients in a basin, except the soda. Warm the milk in a small pan, add the soda to it, and stir quickly. Moisten the mixture with this, and half fill small greased cups or dariole moulds. Cover with greased paper, and steam for one hour. Turn out, and serve with Orange or Lemon Sauce (Recipes 120, 119).

BAKED PUDDINGS.

Apple Dumplings.
Apple Tart.
Apple Tart with Meringue.
Apples à la Madame.
Banana and Damson Tart.
Bread and Cherry Pudding.
Brown Betty.
Chocolate Cheese Cakes.
Lemon Curd Cheese Cakes.
Macaroon Cheese Cakes.
Potato Cheese Cakes.
Cottage Pudding.
Empress Pudding.
Ginger Tartlets.
Gooseberry Pudding.
Jam Puffs.
Jam Roly-Poly.
Open Jam Tart.
Lemon Pudding.
Maids of Honour.
Marrow Pudding.
Mimosa Puddings.
Mincemeat.
Mince Pies.
Orange Pudding.
Orange Slices.
Puff Pastry.
Saucer Puddings.
Short-crust.

Strawberry Short-cake.
Swiss Roll.
Tartlet Cases.
Rhubarb Tartlets.
Strawberry, Raspberry, or Red Currant Tartlets.
Walnut Pudding.
West Riding Pudding.
Winifred's Pudding.

40.—SMALL APPLE DUMPLINGS.

Ingredients—

Short Crust (Recipe 68).　　1 oz. Butter.
6 Apples.　　Grated Rind of ½
1½ oz. Demerara Sugar.　　Lemon.

Method—

Roll out some short crust rather thinly, and cut out six rounds about six inches in diameter with a cutter or saucepan lid.   Wet round the edge of these rounds with cold water, and place an apple peeled and cored whole in the centre of each.   Put the butter, sugar, and grated lemon rind on to a plate, and mix them together with a knife.   Fill up the holes in the apples with this mixture.   Draw up the edges of the pastry so that they meet on the top of the apple, and roll the apple in the hands to make it a good shape.   Place the apple balls as they are ready on a wetted baking tin with the join downwards, brush them over with water or slightly beaten white of egg, and dredge with sugar.   Bake in a moderate oven from twenty to thirty minutes.   When ready, the apples should be soft, and the pastry nicely browned.   Serve hot or cold on a dish with a dish-paper on it, and dredge again with sugar.

NOTE.—Ground cloves, ginger, or cinnamon may be used for flavouring the butter and sugar instead of lemon rind.

41.—APPLE TART.

Ingredients—

Short Crust.	$\frac{1}{4}$ lb. Sugar.
$1\frac{1}{2}$ lbs. Apples.	A little grated Lemon
2 tablespoonfuls Water.	Rind or 3 or 4 Cloves.

Method—

Wipe the apples with a damp cloth, then peel and cut them in quarters. Remove the cores and slice them very thinly. Put them into a pie-dish in alternate layers with the sugar, making the last layer apples. Season with grated lemon rind or a few cloves and add the water. Have the fruit piled high and well away from the sides of the dish. Make some short crust (Recipe 68), and roll it out rather thinly. Wet round the edges of the pie-dish with cold water. Cut a strip an inch wide off the pastry, and lay it round the dish. Press it well on, and where there is a join, wet one of the edges with cold water and press the two together. Then wet round again with cold water, and lay on a piece of pastry large enough to cover the top. Ease this on slightly, and press the two edges well together. With a sharp knife cut off the larger pieces of pastry hanging round the dish, then hold up the dish in the right hand, and with the left trim neatly round the edges. When cutting, take sharp quick strokes, cutting always from you, and slanting the knife outwards from the dish to avoid cutting the pastry too close. Then with the back of the knife mark round the edges of the pastry. Make the marks quite close together, and as neat as possible. Next flute round the edges by drawing the knife quickly upwards and towards you, and being careful to make the flutes an equal distance apart.

Brush the pie over with beaten white of egg or a little cold water, and dredge well with sugar. This is to glaze it, and should be done just before the pie is put in the oven. Then with a skewer make four small holes at the sides of the pie, to allow the steam to escape while cooking. Bake in a moderate oven about one hour, or until the apples are cooked and the pastry is nicely browned. The apples may be tested by running a skewer into the tart and feeling if they are soft. When ready, lift out of the oven and wipe the dish well with a damp cloth. Sprinkle the tart with castor sugar, and serve either hot or cold.

NOTE.—Any other fruit tart may be made in the same way. All fruit must be carefully prepared before being used, and sugar added according to the acidity of the fruit. A mixture of fruits may also be used.

42.—APPLE TART WITH MERINGUE.

Ingredients—   SHORT CRUST.

¼ lb. Butter.	½ teaspoonful Baking
6 oz. Flour.	Powder.
2 oz. Corn Flour.	A squeeze of Lemon
1 oz. Sugar.	Juice.
1 yolk of Egg.	Cold Water.

APPLE MIXTURE.

1 lb. Apples (weighed after peeling).	¼ lb. Sugar.
The Rind of ½ Lemon.	2 or 3 tablespoonfuls Water.

2 yolks of Eggs.

MERINGUE.

3 whites of Eggs.	3 oz. Castor Sugar.

Method—

First make some short crust with the ingredients given above, and according to directions given in Recipe 68. Wet a dish with cold water, and cover it with the pastry rolled out rather thinly. Trim round the edges, and prick all over the foot with a fork. Then roll out the scraps of pastry and cut from it bands about two inches in width. Wet round the pastry covering the edge of the dish, and lay the band round. Where there is a join, wet one edge with cold water, and fix the two pieces as neatly as possible. Then decorate round the edges according to taste, and bake the pastry in a moderate oven for about half an hour, until the pastry is brown and crisp. Meanwhile prepare the apple mixture. Peel the apples, and then weigh them. Slice them thinly, and put them into a stewpan with the sugar, lemon rind, and a very little water. Allow them to stew slowly until quite soft and pulpy, and rub them through a hair or wire sieve. Add to them the two yolks of eggs, and put the mixture into the covered dish. Whip the whites of eggs to a stiff froth, add the sugar sifted to them, and pile this roughly on the top of the apples. Dredge a little sugar over, and return the tart to a slow oven to dry and brown the meringue. About fifteen minutes will be required. This tart may be served hot or cold.

43.—APPLES À LA MADAME.

Ingredients—

6 Apples.	2 oz. Sugar.
2 Eggs.	2 oz. Macaroon-crumbs.
1 gill of Milk.	2 oz. Butter.

Method—

Peel the apples, cut them in thin slices, and stamp out the cores with a small cutter. Butter a pie-dish or fireproof dish, and lay the apples in it in layers, with the macaroon-crumbs and sugar. Pour over all the remainder of the butter melted, and bake in a hot oven until the apples are tender. Beat up the eggs, add the milk and a little sugar, and pour this custard over the apples. Return to the oven until a golden colour, and serve hot, sprinkled with sugar.

44.—BANANA AND DAMSON TART.

Ingredients—

1 lb. Damsons.	½ lb. Sugar.
5 or 6 Bananas.	Short Crust.

Method—

Pick and wash the damsons. Peel and slice the bananas. Arrange these in alternate layers in a pie-dish, sprinkle them rather generously with sugar, and pile the fruit high in the centre. Then add half-gill of cold water or a little liqueur, and cover and bake the tart according to directions given for Apple Tart (Recipe 41).

This is rather a good combination of fruits to use
for a tart. The damsons being acid, supply the flavour
that is wanting in the bananas.

Bottled damsons may be used instead of fresh ones,
but in this case, use some of the syrup instead of
adding water.

45.—BREAD AND CHERRY PUDDING.

Ingredients—

3 gills of Milk.	1 lb. Cherries.
2 oz. Bread-crumbs.	A little grated Lemon
2 oz. Sugar.	Rind.
1 oz. Butter.	3 oz. Sugar.
2 Eggs.	½ cupful of Water.

Juice of ½ Lemon.

Method—

Wash and pick the cherries. Put them into a
saucepan with the water, sugar, and lemon juice, and
stew them until quite tender.

In another saucepan put the milk, the butter, and
the bread-crumbs, and stir over the fire until boiling.
Cook gently for a few minutes until the bread-crumbs
swell, and then remove the pan from the fire, add
the sugar, yolks of eggs, and a little grated lemon rind,
mix well, and lastly add the whites of eggs beaten to
a stiff froth. Mix these in very lightly, breaking them
down as little as possible.

Put the stewed cherries at the foot of a greased pie-
dish, and pour the bread-crumb mixture over them.
Bake in a moderate oven for about half-hour, or until
the pudding is set and nicely browned. Sprinkle
with sugar before serving.

46.—BROWN BETTY.

Ingredients—

6 oz. browned Bread-crumbs.	2 tablespoonfuls Golden Syrup.
1½ lbs. Apples.	½ teaspoonful Cinnamon.
2 oz. Butter.	

1 gill of Water.

Method—

Peel, core, and slice the apples thinly, and put a layer of them at the foot of a pie-dish. Sprinkle some of the bread-crumbs over this, and lay on a few small pieces of butter. Then put in more apples, and repeat these alternate layers until all the apples and bread-crumbs are used up. The last layer must be bread-crumbs. Mix the syrup, water, and cinnamon together, and pour it over the top. Sprinkle with sugar, and put some more butter on the top. Place the pudding in a tin containing hot water, and bake in a moderate oven for one hour, or until the apples are soft. Serve with cream or milk.

47.—CHOCOLATE CHEESE CAKES.

Ingredients—

3 Macaroons.	1 dessert-spoonful Castor Sugar.
1 tablespoonful grated Chocolate.	A few drops of Vanilla.
½ pint Milk.	Short Crust or Puff Pastry.
2 yolks of Eggs.	

Method—

Roll out some short crust or puff pastry rather thinly, and stamp out rounds with a pastry cutter. Line slightly greased patty tins with these, and prick them

D

at the foot to prevent the pastry rising. (The rounds of pastry should be cut rather larger than the diameter of the tins, to allow of some being taken up in the depth.) Put the chocolate into a saucepan with the milk, and let them simmer for about ten minutes over the fire; then add the macaroons crushed to a powder, and simmer a few minutes longer. Remove the pan from the fire, and add the sugar, flavouring, and yolks of eggs. Mix well, and fill the lined tins with this mixture. Lay some narrow strips of pastry in a trellis-work pattern over the top, wetting one edge of pastry wherever a join is made. Bake in a good oven for about twenty minutes; then brush the tartlets over with slightly beaten white of egg, and sprinkle them with sugar.

48.—LEMON CURD CHEESE CAKES.

Ingredients—

½ lb. Castor Sugar.	3 yolks of Eggs.
3 oz. Butter.	2 whites of Eggs.
2 Lemons.	Pastry Cases (Recipe
2 Finger Biscuits.	71).

Method—

Sieve the sugar on to a plate, grate the lemon rind on the top of it, and work the two together with a knife until of a uniform yellow colour. Then put this sugar into a saucepan with the butter and eggs slightly beaten and the finger biscuits made into crumbs. Stir all gently over a slow fire until the mixture thickens and becomes like honey. Then pour into jars, and cover tightly with parchment paper. If stored in a cool place, this will keep for some time.

When tartlets are wanted, fill pastry cases with the mixture, and warm in the oven, or they may be served cold.

Or this Lemon Mixture may be used instead of jam for an open tart.

49.—MACAROON CHEESE CAKES.

Ingredients—

6 oz. Castor Sugar.
3 oz. Sweet Almonds (ground).
3 to 4 whites of Eggs.
Short Crust or Puff Pastry.

A little Jam.
A squeeze of Lemon Juice or 1 teaspoonful Orange-flower Water.

Method—

Sieve the sugar into a basin, and add the ground almonds to it, with a good squeeze of lemon or the orange-flower water. Then add three or four whites of eggs, according to size, and beat them with a wooden spoon or spatula. The mixture must be of a creamy consistency. Line some patty tins with pastry according to Recipe 47, and put a little jam at the foot of each. Then fill them up with the almond mixture. Lay two thin strips of pastry across the top, and dredge the tartlets with sugar, which will give them a cracked appearance when baked. Bake in a rather slow oven about three-quarters of an hour. If baked too quickly, they will rise and then fall again. When ready, they should be nicely browned, and feel firm to the touch. This amount of mixture should fill twelve cases.

50.—POTATO CHEESE CAKES.

Ingredients—

3 oz. Castor Sugar.	3 oz. cooked and sieved
Rind and juice of 1 Orange.	Potato.
	2 oz. Butter.
Rind and juice of ½ Lemon.	2 yolks of Eggs.
	1 white of Egg.

Method—

Grate the rind from one orange and half a lemon, and rub it well into the sugar. Then cream the butter and sugar together in a basin, add the potato and yolks of eggs, then the orange and lemon juice, and lastly the white of egg beaten to a stiff froth.

Line some (about one dozen) patty tins with pastry, the same as for Chocolate Cheese Cakes (Recipe 47), three-quarters fill them with the mixture, and bake about twenty minutes in a good oven.

51.—COTTAGE PUDDING.

Ingredients—

½ lb. Flour.	2 oz. Butter.
1 teaspoonful Baking Powder.	1 gill of Milk.
	1 Egg.
3 oz. Sugar.	A pinch of Salt.

Method—

Sieve the flour, salt, and baking powder on to a piece of paper. Cream the butter and sugar together in a basin, and add the egg to them with a little of the flour. Then add the rest of the flour gradually with the milk, and beat all well together for a few minutes. Pour the mixture into a greased mould,

and bake about half an hour in a moderate oven.
Turn out and serve with Chocolate Sauce (Recipe 115)
or a purée of fruit.

52.—EMPRESS PUDDING.

Ingredients—

¼ lb. Carolina Rice.	Grated rind of ½
1 pint Milk.	Lemon.
2 oz. Castor Sugar.	2 or 3 tablespoon-
2 Eggs.	fuls of Jam.
1 oz. Butter.	A little Pastry.

Method—

Wash the rice well in several waters, then put it into
a saucepan with fresh cold water to cover it.   Bring
to the boil, and add the milk and butter.   Simmer
slowly until the rice is quite tender and has absorbed
the milk.   Then add the grated lemon rind, sugar,
and eggs well beaten.   Mix well.   Line a pie-dish
with pastry according to directions given for West
Riding Pudding (No. 76).   Put the jam at the foot
of the dish, and pour the rice mixture on the top.
Bake in a moderate oven from a half to three-quarters
of an hour.

53.—GINGER TARTLETS.

Ingredients—

Short Crust.	1 oz. Rice-flour.
1 Egg.	½ teaspoonful Baking
2 oz. Butter.	Powder.
2 oz. Sugar.	1 dessertspoonful Syrup
1 oz. Flour.	from Ginger.

2 oz. Preserved Ginger.

Method—

Roll out some short crust rather thinly, and stamp out eight or nine rounds with a pastry cutter slightly larger than the top of the patty tins to be used. Grease the patty tins and line them with the pastry. Press the pastry well on to the sides and bottom of the tins, and then prick each one at the foot with a fork.

To Make the Mixture.—Cream the butter and sugar together in a basin, add the yolk of egg and ginger syrup, then both kinds of flour, sieved, mix well, and lastly add the ginger cut in small pieces, the baking powder and white of egg beaten to a stiff froth. Half fill the lined tins with this mixture, and bake them in a good oven about twenty minutes. When ready, they should feel firm to the touch, and be nicely browned. Dredge them with sugar, and remove them from the tins.

NOTE.—For short crust see Recipe 68.

54.—BAKED GOOSEBERRY PUDDING.

Ingredients—

1 lb. Gooseberries.	Suet Pastry or Short Crust
5 or 6 oz. Sugar.	(Recipes 35, 68).

Method—

First top and tail the gooseberries, and wash them well. Then make the pastry according to Recipe 35 or 68. Roll out the pastry to rather less than quarter-inch in thickness, grease a basin and line it with it, pressing it well on to the sides, and keeping it of a uniform thickness. Cut off the trimmings of the pastry, and roll them out in a round shape large enough to cover the pudding. Fill up the basin with

the gooseberries and sugar, pressing them well in, as
the fruit sinks considerably in cooking. Wet the edge
of the pastry which lines the basin with cold water,
put on the top, and press the two edges well together.
Twist a piece of greased paper over the top of the
basin, and bake the pudding in a moderate oven for
at least one hour. Then turn out on a hot dish, and
sprinkle with sugar.

55.—JAM PUFFS.

Required—

Pastry.	White of Egg.
Jam.	Castor Sugar.

Method—

Almost any pastry may be used for these (see
Recipes 66, 68), or scraps of the same. Roll out the
pastry rather thinly, and with a round cutter four or five
inches in diameter stamp out rounds. Wet half-way
round the edges of these with a little cold water, and
put a small portion of jam in the centre of each.
Double over and press the edges well together, and
mark round with the end of a small teaspoon. Place
the puffs on a greased or wetted baking tin, brush
them over with some beaten white of egg or water,
and dredge with sugar. Bake in a moderate oven
from fifteen to twenty minutes until nicely browned.
When ready, dredge again with sugar, and serve hot
or cold.

NOTES.—These may be made triangular in shape
by cutting the pastry in squares instead of rounds and
doubling the pieces over from corner to corner, or
round by putting one small round on the top of
another with the jam between.

56.—JAM ROLY-POLY (BAKED).

Make in the same way as boiled roly-poly (Recipe 24). When ready, place it on a greased tin with the join downwards. Brush over with a little water, and sprinkle with sugar. Bake in a moderate oven from one to one and a half hours, or until thoroughly cooked and nicely browned. Serve on a hot dish, with a dish-paper under it, and sprinkle with sugar.

57.—OPEN JAM TART.

Required—
Pastry. | Jam.

Method—

Make some Short Crust or Puff Pastry (Recipes 68, 66), and roll it out rather thinly. Wet a flat dish with cold water, press the pastry well into the shape of the dish, and trim round the edges with a knife. Prick the pastry lining the foot of the dish with a fork, to prevent it rising while baking, and spread with jam. Roll out the trimmings of pastry and cut off some narrow strips. Twist these, and lay them across the tart in a trellis-work pattern. Wet the edges with cold water, and lay a broader band of pastry round. Mark this with a knife, or snip it with a pair of scissors, and flute round the edges with a knife. Bake the tart in a moderate oven from thirty to forty minutes, or until well cooked and nicely browned.

NOTES.—The tart may be baked without the jam, and some pastry leaves made and baked and used for decorating afterwards. Any nice stewed fruit may be used instead of jam. If the tart is served cold, it may be decorated with a little whipped cream.

58.—LEMON PUDDING.

Ingredients—

Short Crust (Recipe 68).	2 Eggs.
2 oz. Butter.	2 oz. Bread or Cake
2 oz. Sugar.	crumbs.
1 Lemon.	¼ teasp. Baking Powder.

Method—

Line a dish (about ten inches in length) with short crust according to directions given for Open Tart (Recipe 57), and then prepare the mixture.

Grate the rind off the lemon as lightly as possible, and put it into a basin with the sugar and butter. Beat these together with a wooden spoon until of a creamy consistency. Add one egg and half the crumbs and beat well, then the second egg and the remainder of the crumbs. Strain in the lemon juice, add the baking powder free from lumps, and mix again. Spread this mixture over the lined dish, keeping it well off the edges, put a few leaves or fancy-shaped pieces of pastry on the top, and bake in a moderate oven from half to three-quarters of an hour.

Sprinkle with sugar before serving.

NOTE.—If liked, a little jam may be spread over the pastry before the mixture.

59.—MAIDS OF HONOUR.

Ingredients—

1 pint Milk ⎫ Curd.	The grated rind of ½
1 des.-sp. Rennet ⎭	Lemon.
2 yolks of Eggs.	A pinch of Nutmeg.
½ gill clotted Cream.	2 oz. Currants.
2 oz. Sugar.	½ glass of Brandy.
A pinch of Cinnamon.	Puff Pastry (Recipe 66).

Method—

Warm the milk slightly and turn it with the rennet. When the curd has formed, put it in a coarse cloth on a sieve, and drain for twelve hours. Next day press the curd lightly with the cloth, and then put it in a basin. Add to it the yolks of eggs, sugar, cream, currants well cleaned, brandy and flavourings, and mix all together.

Line from ten to twelve patty pans with puff pastry rolled out rather thinly. Prick them well at the foot with a fork, and fill them with the above mixture. Bake them from fifteen to twenty minutes in a good oven, and sprinkle with sugar.

NOTE.—The currants may be replaced by a few blanched and chopped almonds.

60.—MARROW PUDDING.

Ingredients—

1 teacupful Bread-crumbs.	2 oz. Sugar.
	A pinch of Nutmeg.
1 pint Milk.	A pinch of Cinnamon.
4 oz. Beef Marrow.	1 oz. Currants.
2 Eggs.	1 oz. stoned Raisins.

A little Pastry.

Method—

Put the bread-crumbs into a basin, boil the milk, and pour it over them. Cover the basin with a plate, and allow this to stand for half an hour. Meanwhile edge a pie-dish with pastry according to directions given in Recipe 41, and decorate it neatly. When the bread-crumbs are thoroughly soaked, add to them the marrow finely shred, the sugar, fruit, spice, and yolks of eggs, mix all together, and lastly stir in the whites of eggs beaten to a stiff froth. Pour this mixture into the prepared pie-dish, and bake in a good oven from twenty-five to thirty minutes. Sprinkle with sugar before serving.

NOTE.—Cherries or candied peel and almonds may replace the currants and raisins.

61.—MIMOSA PUDDINGS.

Ingredients—

5 oz. Bread-crumbs.	1 oz. Citron Peel.
2 Eggs.	1 teaspoonful Orange-
3 oz. Butter.	flower Water.
3 oz. Castor Sugar.	

Method—

Sieve the sugar into a basin, add the butter, and beat these two together with a wooden spoon until very soft and creamy. Add the eggs one at a time with some of the bread-crumbs, and beat well between each. Then beat all together, and add the flavouring. Grease some small tins or moulds, and sprinkle at the foot of each some finely-chopped citron peel. Half fill them with the mixture, and bake in a good oven about fifteen minutes. Serve with Custard Sauce (Recipe 116).

62.—MINCEMEAT.

Ingredients—

½ lb. Suet.	3 oz. Citron Peel.
½ lb. Valencia Raisins.	3 oz. Lemon Peel.
½ lb. Sultana Raisins.	3 oz. Orange Peel.
½ lb. Currants.	6 oz. Sweet Almonds.
½ lb. Figs.	1 dessertspoonful Mixed
½ lb. Apples.	Spices.
1 lb. Sugar.	Rind and juice of 2
2 tablespoonfuls Mar-	Lemons.
malade.	2 glasses of Brandy.

1 glass of Rum.

Method—

First prepare the fruit, and as each article is ready put it into a large crock or basin. Pick and clean the currants and sultanas. Stone the raisins, peel and core the apples, and chop these two together with a long sharp knife. Shred the peel finely, and blanch and chop the almonds. Remove the stalks from the figs, wash them in very hot water, and then dry and cut them in small pieces. Add the spice to the fruit, also the suet finely chopped. and the lemon rind grated, and mix thoroughly with the hands. Then add the marmalade, lemon juice, rum, and brandy, and mix again. Cover and stand in a cool place for twenty-four hours. Then mix once more, and pack into pots or jars. Tie a piece of parchment over the top of the pots to make them perfectly air-tight, and keep the mincemeat in a cool place. Do not use for several weeks.

NOTE.—This mincemeat will keep quite good for a year at least. If it should become rather dry, more wine or spirit may be added.

63.—MINCE PIES.

Required—

Puff Pastry (Recipe 66).   Mincemeat (Recipe 62).

Method—

Roll out puff pastry to one-eighth of an inch in thickness, and stamp out rounds with a cutter three to four inches in diameter.   Fold up the scraps of pastry and roll them out again, cutting out more rounds as before.   (The first rounds that are cut out are always the best, so keep them more especially for the top of the pies.)   Wet round the edge of half the number of rounds with a little cold water, and put a good teaspoonful of mincemeat in the centre of each. Cover with the other rounds of pastry, and press the two edges well together.   Make a small hole with a skewer on the top of each pie, brush them over wiht slightly beaten white of egg, and dredge them with sugar.   Place the pies on a wetted baking sheet, and bake in a good oven for twenty minutes until the pastry is well risen and nicely browned.   When ready, sprinkle again with sugar and serve hot.

64.—ORANGE PUDDING (BAKED).

Ingredients—

2 oz. Cake-crumbs.	2 Eggs.
2 oz. Castor Sugar.	1 gill Milk.
1 oz. Butter.	2 Oranges.

A little Pastry.

Method—

Line a medium-sized pie-dish with pastry according to Recipe 76, and then prepare the mixture.   Wipe the oranges with a damp cloth, and grate off the rind on the top of the sugar. Work the rind into the sugar with a broad-bladed knife until they are of a uniform yellow colour. Then put this into a basin, and add the cake-crumbs sieved and the butter broken in pieces. Heat the milk in a small saucepan, and pour it over the crumbs, &c. Stir until the butter is melted, add the yolks of eggs, the strained juice of oranges, and lastly the whites of eggs beaten to a stiff froth. Mix lightly, and pour all into the prepared dish. Bake in a moderate oven until set and of a light brown colour. It will take about three-quarters of an hour. Sprinkle with sugar and serve hot.

65.—ORANGE SLICES.

Ingredients—

1 Orange.	1½ gills of Milk.
2 oz. Sugar.	2 yolks of Eggs.
1 oz. Corn-flour.	Puff Pastry.

Method—

To make the mixture, add the milk gradually to the corn-flour, mixing until smooth. Turn this into a small saucepan, and stir over the fire until boiling. Grate the rind from the orange and rub it into the sugar. Add this orange sugar to the corn-flour with the strained juice and yolks of eggs. Cook the mixture for a minute or two longer over the fire, and then turn it into a basin to cool. Roll out some puff pastry into an oblong-shaped piece and rather thin. Spread one half of it with the above orange mixture, wet round the edges and fold the other piece of pastry over, pressing the two edges well together. Brush over the surface with slightly beaten white of egg, and dredge well with sugar. With a sharp knife cut the pastry into finger-shaped pieces, and place them carefully on a wetted baking tin. Bake in a good oven from fifteen to twenty minutes, and sprinkle again with sugar while still hot.

66.—PUFF PASTRY (Fr. Feuilletage).

Proportion—

½ lb. Flour.	A squeeze of Lemon
½ lb. Butter.	Juice.
A pinch of Salt.	Cold Water.

Method—

Weigh the butter, and let it lie in a basin of cold water for some time before using it. Sieve the flour and salt into a clean dry basin, and add the lemon juice to them. Lift the butter out of the cold water and dry it lightly in a floured cloth. Take a quarter of the butter, and rub it into the flour with the tips of the fingers and thumbs until there are no lumps left. Then mix with cold water into a stiffish dough. Turn this on to a floured board and work it well with the hands until it will no longer stick to the fingers and forms a perfectly smooth dough. Then roll it rather thinly into a square or round shape. The butter to be used should be as nearly as possible of the same consistency as the paste. Form it into a neat flat cake, and place it in the centre of the pastry. Fold it up rather loosely, and flatten the folds with a rolling pin. Then roll out the pastry into a long narrow strip, being careful that the butter does not break through. Fold it exactly in three, press down the folds, and lay the pastry aside in a cool place for a quarter of an hour at least. This is called giving the pastry one "turn," and seven of these is the number usually required for puff pastry. The next time the pastry is rolled, place it with the joins at your right-hand side, and the open ends towards you. Give it two "turns" this time, and again set it aside in a cool place for at least fifteen minutes. Repeat this until the pastry has had seven rolls in all, one roll or turn the first time, and after that, two each time with an interval between. The object of this cooling between the rolls is to keep the butter and flour in distinct and separate layers, in which it is the function of the rolling pin and folding to arrange them, and on which the lightness of the pastry depends. When rolling, keep the pressure of the two hands as equal as possible. If the pastry becomes rounded, it shows that there is more pressure being done on the rounded side than the other. After it has received its last roll, it is better to be laid aside for some time before using it, then roll to the thickness required. This pastry will keep for several days in cold weather if wrapped in a piece of well-greased paper.

67.—SAUCER PUDDINGS.

Ingredients—

2 oz. Butter.	2 oz. Flour.
3 oz. Sugar.	½ pint Milk.
2 Eggs.	A little Flavouring.

Some Jam.

Method—

Sieve the sugar into a basin, add the butter, and beat these two together with a wooden spoon until of a creamy consistency. Then add the yolks of eggs,

half the flour, and a few drops of any flavouring that
is liked.   Beat well, add the milk, and then stir in
very lightly the whites of eggs beaten to a stiff froth
and the remainder of the flour.   Have ready four or
five saucers or some large patty tins well greased; fill
them with the mixture, and bake in a moderate oven
from fifteen to twenty minutes.   Turn one of these
puddings out on a hot dish, cover it with jam heated
until almost liquid, lay another pudding on the top,
then more jam, and so on until all are used.   Sift
sugar over the top, and serve at once.

68.—SHORT CRUST.

Proportions—

½ lb. Flour.	¼ lb. Butter.
1 teaspoonful Castor Sugar.	A squeeze of Lemon Juice.

Cold Water.

Method—

Rub the flour and sugar through a wire sieve into
a clean dry basin.   Add a squeeze of lemon juice, and
if fresh butter is being used, a pinch of salt also.   Put
in the butter, cover it well over with the flour, and
break it in pieces.   Then rub together lightly with the
tips of the fingers and thumbs until as fine as bread-
crumbs.   While rubbing, keep lifting the flour well
up in the basin so that air may mix with it and the
butter is not made too soft.   Then make a well in the
centre of these dry ingredients, and add cold water
very gradually with the left hand whilst mixing with
the right.   Mix with the hand or with a knife.   Use
very little water in the mixing of this paste or it will
be tough instead of short.   Flour the pastry board

E

slightly, lay the dough on it, and work lightly with the hands until free from cracks. Then flour a rolling pin, press down the pastry first, then with sharp quick strokes roll it out to the thickness required. This pastry only requires one roll. Roll it on the one side only, and be careful it does not stick to the board. Lift it gently at the sides from time to time, and dust a little flour under and over as required. Use no more flour than is necessary for this purpose, as too much will make the pastry hard.

NOTES.—The above is a fairly rich paste, and if a plainer one is wished, use only 3 oz. of butter, or substitute lard or dripping for the butter.

The pastry may be made richer by using rather more butter, 6 oz. to ½ lb. flour, and the yolk of an egg beaten up with a little water for mixing.

The quantities given will make a pastry quite suitable for all ordinary purposes.

This is one of the most wholesome kinds of pastry. The butter is so thoroughly mixed with the flour, that the latter is more thoroughly cooked and is more digestible than in some of the Flaky Pastries.

69.—STRAWBERRY SHORT-CAKE.

Ingredients—

½ lb. Flour.	1 oz. Butter.
1½ teaspoonfuls Baking Powder.	Milk.
½ teaspoonful Salt.	1 lb. Strawberries.
	½ lb. Castor Sugar.

3 whites of Eggs.

Method—

Sieve the baking powder and salt with the flour, and rub in the butter until free from lumps. Then

stir in lightly and quickly sufficient milk to make a
soft dough—too soft to roll. Turn it into a flat round
tin that has been greased and floured, and bake in a
hot oven about thirty minutes. Then unmould, cut
a circle around the top of the cake within one inch of
the edge, and lift off the circle of crust. With a fork
pick out the crumb from the centre, being careful not
to break through the sides. Crush the strawberries
slightly, and sprinkle them with half the sugar. Let
them stand for half an hour, and strain off some of the
juice. Fill up the cake with the strawberries, and
replace the circle of crust. Whip the whites of eggs
to a stiff froth, and add the remainder of the sugar to
them. Heap this meringue irregularly on the top of
the cake. (A forcing bag may be used to give it a
more ornamental form.) Place it in the oven for
a minute or two to slightly colour the meringue.
Sprinkle with sugar, and decorate with a few whole
strawberries. Serve the juice from the strawberries
as a sauce.

NOTES.—Short-cake should be freshly made and
used as soon as possible.

Whipped cream may be used instead of the
meringue.

70.—SWISS ROLL.

Ingredients—

3 Eggs.
The weight of 3 Eggs
  in Flour and Castor
  Sugar.
The weight of 2 Eggs
  in Butter.

½ teaspoonful Baking
  Powder.
A few drops of Fla-
  vouring.
2 or 3 tablespoonfuls
  Jam.

Method—

Sieve the sugar into a clean dry basin, add the butter to it, and beat these two together with a wooden spoon until they are of a creamy consistency. (If the butter is very hard, the basin may be stood for a minute or two over a pan of hot water or at the entrance to the oven.) Then add one egg and a little of the flour sieved, beat well, and add another egg and a little more flour, beat again, and add the last egg and the remainder of the flour. The lightness of the roll depends upon the mixture being well beaten. Flavour to taste, and add the baking powder last. Spread the mixture on a flat tin of an oblong shape that has been lined with paper. (The mixture should not be more than a quarter of an inch in thickness, or it will not roll when baked.) Bake in a quick oven for about fifteen minutes, or until nicely browned and firm to the touch. Have ready a sheet of paper sprinkled with sugar, and turn the pastry on to it. Trim the edges with a sharp knife, and spread quickly with the jam slightly warmed. Then take hold of one end of the paper and roll quickly and carefully up. Serve with Custard Sauce (Recipe 116) poured round.

NOTE.—This is also served as a cake when cold.

71.—TARTLET CASES.

In families where there are unexpected visitors, it is a good plan to keep some tartlet cases ready at hand. With some fresh fruit or preserve they make a nice sweet for an emergency. Grease any small patty tins or quenelle-shaped moulds, and line them with rounds

of short crust rolled out rather thinly. Press the
pastry well into the moulds so that it may take the
exact shape, and prick it all over the foot to prevent it
blistering while baking. Lay a small round of paper
into each, and fill with rice or small beans. Bake in
a moderate oven until the pastry is dry and nicely
browned. Then remove the tartlets from the tins,
empty them of the rice or beans, and store them in
an air-tight tin until wanted. The pastry for these
should be rather stiff and not too rich.

The cases may be filled with a little jam or fresh
fruit (see Recipe 73), and some whipped and sweetened
cream may be piled on the top.

72.—RHUBARB TARTLETS.

Ingredients—

  1 bunch of Rhubarb. | Sugar.
                 Short Crust (Recipe 68).

Method—

Wipe the rhubarb with a damp cloth. If old, skin
it, and cut it into small pieces.

Roll out the pastry to one eighth of an inch in
thickness. Cut out from ten to twelve rounds with a
pastry cutter, and put them to one side. Roll out
the pastry again, and cut out more rounds, repeating
this until you have other ten or twelve rounds. Grease
some small patty tins, and line them with the rounds
of pastry that were last cut out, as they are never quite
so good as the first cuttings from the pastry. Fill up
with rhubarb and sugar, wet round the edge of the
pastry lining the tins with cold water, and put the
best rounds on the top. Press the two edges of pastry

well together, and make a small hole with a skewer on the top of each tartlet. Brush them over with water or white of egg, dredge with sugar, and bake in a good moderate oven for twenty minutes. They should be a nice brown colour. Should they become too brown before the pastry is cooked, cover with paper. When ready, sprinkle again with sugar, and remove from the tins.

73.—STRAWBERRY, RASPBERRY, OR RED CURRANT TARTLETS.

Required—

½ pint Fruit.
A little Liqueur or any Fruit Syrup.

¼ lb. Sugar.
1 dozen Tartlet Cases (Recipe 71).

½ gill of Water.

Method—

Choose nice ripe fruit, pick it, and put it into a basin. Put the sugar and water into a saucepan, and boil them to a syrup, but do not let them colour. Add a little liqueur or some fruit syrup or essence to flavour. Pour this syrup over the fruit, and stand in a warm place for half hour. Then lift out the fruit carefully, place it in the tartlet cases, and pour one or two teaspoonfuls of the syrup over. Serve either hot or cold.

74.—RICE AND CHERRY PIE.

Ingredients—

¼ lb. Rice.
¼ lb. Sugar.
1 pint Water.
1 Vanilla Pod.
1 lb. Cherries

Short Crust or Puff Pastry.
1 tablespoonful Biscuit-crumbs.
A little white of Egg.

Method—

First put the sugar, vanilla, and water into a saucepan, bring them to the boil, and boil for ten minutes. Then add the rice well washed, and stew it until quite soft and pulpy. Stalk and stone the cherries, and break a few of the stones and blanch the kernels. Put a quarter of the cherries at the foot of a pie-dish and sprinkle a few kernels over them, cover this with a quarter of the rice, and repeat these layers until the rice and fruit are all used up, being careful to pile it all well in the centre. Cover the pie according to directions given in Recipe 41, and have the pastry rather thin. Bake the pie in a moderate oven for one hour, then brush it over with slightly beaten white of egg, and sprinkle it with sugar and biscuit-crumbs (preferably macaroon-crumbs). Return to the oven for a few minutes longer, and serve hot.

NOTE.—Any fruit may be used for this kind of pie, and the flavouring may be varied.

75.—WALNUT PUDDING.

Ingredients—

¼ lb. Bread-crumbs.	2 Eggs.
¼ lb. shelled Walnuts.	A little grated Lemon
2 oz. Sugar.	Rind.

1 pint Milk.

Method—

Put the bread-crumbs and sugar into a basin with a little grated lemon rind. Heat the milk, and pour it over them. Toast the walnuts in the oven for a few minutes, then pound them in a mortar or chop them finely. Add them to the bread-crumbs, &c.,

with the yolks of eggs, and mix well. Whisk the whites of eggs to a stiff froth, and stir them in lightly at the last. Pour the mixture into a greased pie-dish, and bake in a moderate oven for half an hour, or until brown and well risen.

NOTES.—The pie-dish may be lined with pastry before putting in the mixture, (see Recipe 76). A little strawberry or any nice jam may be put into the dish first.

76.—WEST RIDING PUDDING.

Ingredients—

2 Eggs.	Some scraps of Pastry.
The weight of the Eggs in Butter, Flour, and Sugar.	¼ teaspoonful Baking Powder.
	A little Flavouring.

2 tablespoonfuls Jam.

Method—

Roll out scraps of any suitable pastry into a strip four or five inches in width, and line the sides and edges of a wetted pie-dish with it. Join the ends neatly, and press the pastry well on to the rim of the dish and slightly over the outer edge; then trim round with a knife. Wet the rim of pastry with a little cold water, and decorate all round the edge with small fancy-shaped pieces of pastry. Press these well on. Put the jam at the foot of the pie-dish, and then prepare the mixture. Sieve the sugar into a basin, add the butter, and beat these two together with a wooden spoon until they are of a creamy consistency. Then add one egg and half the flour sieved, beat well, then the second egg and the rest of the flour, and beat again. Flavour to taste, and add the baking powder at the last. Half fill the pie-dish with this mixture, and bake in a good oven for one hour, or until the mixture is quite set and of a nice brown colour. Sprinkle with sugar before serving.

77.—WINIFRED'S PUDDING.

Ingredients—

1 pint Strawberries or Raspberries.
$\frac{1}{4}$ lb. Sugar.

$\frac{1}{2}$ pint Milk.
2 oz. Bread or Cake Crumbs.

2 Eggs.

Method—

Pick the fruit free from stalks, and put it at the foot of a greased pie-dish. Beat the eggs, and add the milk to them. Put the crumbs and sugar into a basin, and strain the eggs and milk over. Then pour all on the top of the fruit, and wipe round the edges of the pie-dish. Place the pudding in a deep baking tin, surround it with cold water, and bake in a moderate oven about three-quarters of an hour, or until set and nicely browned. Sprinkle with sugar before serving.

NOTE.—This pudding is also nice served cold, when a little whipped and sweetened cream may be piled on the top.

SOUFFLÉS, OMELETS, AND FRITTERS.

Apricot Soufflé (1).
Apricot Soufflé (2, Baked).
Apple Soufflé.
Chocolate Soufflé.
Coffee Soufflé.
Ground-rice Soufflé.
Lemon Soufflé.
Little Ginger Soufflés.
Little Orange Soufflés.
Orange Soufflé.
Orange-flower Water Soufflé.
Pineapple Soufflé.
Prune Soufflé.
Semolina Soufflé.
Vanilla Soufflé.
Omelet Soufflé (1).
Omelet Soufflé (2).
Chocolate Omelet.
Rum Omelet.
Batter for Fritters (1).
Batter for Fritters (2).
Almond Fritters.
American Fritters or Doughnuts.
Apple Fritters.
Banana Fritters.
Beignets Soufflés.
Bread Fritters.

Cherry Fritters.
Orange Fritters.
Pancakes.
Peach or Apricot Fritters.
Pear Fritters.
Rice Croquettes.
Semolina Fritters.

78.—APRICOT SOUFFLÉ.

Ingredients—

1 oz. Butter.	2 or 3 drops of Carmine
1 oz. Flour.	or Cochineal.
1 oz. Castor Sugar.	4 whites of Eggs.
1 gill Apricot Purée.	A pinch of Salt.
3 yolks of Eggs.	A squeeze Lemon Juice.

Method—

First prepare the purée by rubbing some tinned apricots through a hair sieve. Use some of the syrup from the tin along with the apricots so as not to have the purée too thick. Fresh apricots may be used in place of the tinned, but these would require to be stewed first with a little water and sugar.

In making the soufflé, proceed exactly according to directions given for Vanilla Soufflé (Recipe 92), using the gill of apricot purée instead of the gill of milk. Before mixing in the whites, add a squeeze of lemon juice, and just enough carmine or cochineal to make the mixture of a peachy colour. Pour the mixture into a greased soufflé tin (see page viii), cover with greased paper, and steam slowly and steadily from half to three-quarters of an hour, or until the soufflé is well risen and feels firm to the touch. Turn out carefully, and serve at once with Apricot, Custard, or Wine Sauce poured round it.

79.—APRICOT SOUFFLÉ.

(Another Way—Baked.)

Ingredients—

3 oz. Castor Sugar.	4 whites of Eggs.
½ oz. Rice-flour.	5 or 6 tinned Apricots.
1 gill Syrup from Apricots.	Vanilla or other flavouring.
3 yolks of Eggs.	A pinch of Salt.

Method—

Put the yolks of eggs and sugar into a basin, and work them together with a wooden spoon until of a creamy consistency. Then add the rice-flour and the salt, and mix again. Add the apricot syrup by degrees, stirring all the time, and turn the mixture into a saucepan. Cook over a gentle fire, stirring all the time, until almost boiling; then remove at once, and stir until slightly cooled. Add the apricots, cut in small pieces, and the flavouring. A little liqueur, Maraschino or Noyau, is an improvement. Beat the whites to a stiff froth, and stir them lightly in at the last. Arrange the mixture on a flat fire-proof dish in the form of a dome. Mark the sides with the back of a fork, and place in the oven twenty minutes or rather more before serving. Serve on a dish with a folded and warmed serviette under it.

Some Apricot Sauce may be served separately (see Recipe 112).

80.—APPLE SOUFFLÉ (BAKED).

Ingredients—

3 large Apples.   2 oz. Castor Sugar.
2 Eggs.   ½ oz. Butter.
Grated rind of ½ Lemon.

Method—

Bake the apples in the oven until they are thoroughly cooked. Then scoop out all the soft inside and rub this pulp through a hair sieve. Put the sugar, lemon rind, and yolks of eggs into a medium-sized basin, and beat them together with a wooden spoon until of a creamy consistency; then add the apple pulp, and mix all together. Beat the whites of the eggs to a stiff froth, and stir them lightly in at the last. Pour the mixture into a greased china soufflé dish or pie-dish, and bake in a moderate oven for about twenty minutes, or until well risen and firm to the touch. When ready, sprinkle with sugar and serve as quickly as possible.

81.—CHOCOLATE SOUFFLÉ.

Ingredients—

2 or 3 oz. Chocolate.   3 yolks of Eggs.
1 gill of Milk.   4 whites of Eggs.
½ oz. Potato Flour.   A few drops of Vanilla.
1 tablespoonful Cream.   2 oz. Castor Sugar.

Method—

Break the chocolate into small pieces, and put it into an enamelled saucepan with half the milk. Cook gently over the fire, stirring from time to time, until the chocolate is melted and quite free from lumps. Put the sugar, yolks of eggs, and vanilla into a basin, and work them together with a wooden spoon until they are of a creamy consistency. Add the rest of the milk to this, then the chocolate by degrees. Return all to the saucepan, and cook together over the fire until almost boiling. Then remove from the fire, add the cream, and stir occasionally for a few minutes. Beat up the whites of the eggs to a stiff froth, and mix them by degrees with the other mixture, stirring them in as lightly as possible. Pour into a greased soufflé dish, and cook from fifteen to twenty minutes in a good oven. Should the soufflé become too brown, put a piece of paper on the top, but do not open the oven door too often. Sprinkle with a little sugar just before serving, and send to table directly.

82.—COFFEE SOUFFLÉ.

Ingredients.—

1 oz. Butter.	½ gill Cream.
1 oz. Flour.	3 yolks of Eggs.
½ gill strong Coffee.	4 Whites of Eggs.

1 oz. Castor Sugar.

CARAMEL.

3 oz. Loaf Sugar.	A squeeze of Lemon
½ gill Water.	Juice.

Method—

Put the loaf sugar, water, and squeeze of lemon juice into an iron saucepan or sugar-boiler, and cook them until of a golden brown colour. Pour this into an ungreased soufflé tin, take hold of the tin with a cloth, and allow the caramel to run round the sides, coating them well. Cool for a few minutes, and tie a band of greased paper round the outside of the tin (see page viii).

Then proceed to make the soufflé.

Melt the butter in a small stewpan, add the flour, and mix well together with a wooden spoon. Pour in the coffee and cream, and stir over the fire again until the mixture thickens and begins to draw away from the sides of the saucepan. Remove the pan from the fire, and add the sugar and the yolks of eggs, one at a time. Beat the mixture well after each yolk is added. Then beat the whites of eggs to a stiff froth, and stir them lightly in with a metal spoon. Pour the mixture into the prepared mould, cover with greased paper, and steam very slowly from thirty to forty minutes. Turn out carefully on to a hot dish, and serve immediately.

NOTE.—The caramel may be omitted, and the soufflé served with any suitable sauce.

83.—GROUND-RICE SOUFFLÉ.

Ingredients—

1 pint Milk.	1 tablespoonful Sugar.
1 oz. Ground-rice.	1½ oz. Butter.
A pinch of Salt.	3 Eggs.

Vanilla.

Method—

Mix the ground-rice with a little of the milk, and put the rest into a saucepan to heat. When hot, but not boiling, add the ground-rice, and stir over the fire until boiling. Add the sugar and butter, and cook for about ten minutes. Then remove the pan from the fire and stir in the yolks of eggs, flavour with vanilla or any other flavouring preferred, and lastly stir in the whites beaten to a stiff froth. Pour the mixture into a greased pie-dish or fireproof dish, and bake in a moderate oven for twenty minutes. Serve directly, sprinkled with powdered sugar.

84.—LEMON SOUFFLÉ.

Ingredients—

1 oz. Butter.	1 gill of Milk.
1 oz. Flour.	A squeeze of Lemon
1 oz. Castor Sugar.	Juice.
Grated rind of 1	3 yolks of Eggs.
Lemon.	4 whites of Eggs.

A pinch of Salt.

Method—

Melt the butter in a small stewpan, add the flour, and mix well together with a wooden spoon. Pour in the milk, and stir quickly over the fire until the mixture boils and thickens. Wipe the lemon with a damp cloth, and grate the rind very thinly off it on to the top of the sugar. Rub the sugar and lemon rind together with the tips of the fingers until the sugar looks quite yellow. Remove the pan from the fire, and add this sugar and a squeeze of lemon juice, then the yolks one at a time, beating well between each. Add a pinch of salt to the whites, and whisk them to a very stiff froth, then with an iron spoon stir them lightly but thoroughly into the other mixture. Pour all into a prepared soufflé tin (see page viii), cover with greased paper, and steam slowly from thirty to forty minutes, or until firm to the touch. Turn out carefully on to a hot dish, and serve with Custard, Lemon, or Wine Sauce poured round it.

85.—LITTLE GINGER SOUFFLÉS (BAKED).

Ingredients—

1 oz. Butter.	1 oz. Sugar.
½ oz. Corn-flour.	2 yolks of Eggs.
½ gill Milk.	3 whites of Eggs.
½ gill Ginger Syrup.	2 oz. preserved Ginger.

Method—

Melt the butter in an enamelled saucepan, add the milk and corn-flour, and stir over the fire until thick and smooth. Remove the saucepan from the fire, and add the sugar, ginger syrup, and ginger cut in tiny pieces. Mix well, and add the yolks one at a time, beating well between each. Lastly, stir in the whites of the eggs beaten to a stiff froth, mixing them in as lightly as possible. Grease some small china soufflé dishes, three-quarter fill them with the mixture, and bake in a good oven for about fifteen minutes until they are a nice brown colour and well risen. Sprinkle with sugar, and serve immediately.

86.—LITTLE ORANGE SOUFFLÉS.

Ingredients—

3 large Oranges.	1 gill Orange Juice.
1 oz. Butter.	2 yolks of Eggs.
½ oz. Flour.	3 whites of Eggs.

1 dessertspoonful Sugar.

F

Method—

Cut the oranges in halves, and remove all the juice and pith from the insides without destroying the skins. Then melt the butter in a small pan, add the flour, and mix until smooth. Pour in one gill of orange juice (strained), and stir until boiling. Then remove the pan from the fire, add the yolks of eggs, one at a time and the sugar, beat the mixture well, and lastly, add the whites which have been beaten to a stiff froth. Mix them in quickly and lightly, and three-quarter fill the orange skins with this soufflé mixture. Place them on a tin, and bake in a good oven about twenty minutes. Dredge with sugar, and serve as quickly as possible.

87.—ORANGE SOUFFLÉ.

Make in the same way as Lemon Soufflé (Recipe 84), substituting the grated rind of one orange and half the juice in place of lemon rind and juice. Serve with Orange Sauce (Recipe 120).

88.—ORANGE-FLOWER WATER SOUFFLÉ.

Make in the same way as Vanilla Soufflé (Recipe 92), substituting one dessertspoonful orange-flower water for the vanilla. The mould may be caramelled the same as for Coffee Soufflé. Serve with Wine Sauce (see Sauces 126, 127).

89.—PINEAPPLE SOUFFLÉ.

Ingredients—

3 oz. tinned Pineapple.	2 oz. Butter.
1 gill of Syrup from tin.	2 oz. Sugar.
½ gill of Milk.	2 oz. Flour.
A few drops of Carmine.	3 yolks of Eggs.
Flavouring.	4 whites of Eggs.

Method—

Melt the butter in a small stewpan, add the flour, and mix well together with a wooden spoon. Add the pineapple syrup and milk, and stir again over the fire until the mixture thickens and draws away easily from the sides of the saucepan. Then remove the pan from the fire and add the sugar, flavouring to taste, and the pineapple cut in tiny dice. Colour slightly pink with a few drops of carmine. Beat the whites of the eggs to a stiff froth, and stir them lightly in at the last. Pour the mixture into a prepared soufflé tin (page viii), and steam slowly from thirty to forty minutes, or until firm to the touch. Turn out carefully on to a hot dish, and serve with Pineapple Sauce (Recipe 121) poured round it.

90.—PRUNE SOUFFLÉ.

Ingredients—

¼ lb. Prunes.	2 or 3 drops of Carmine.
1 gill Water.	2 Eggs.
2 oz. Sugar.	1 tablespoonful Castor
Juice of ½ Lemon.	Sugar.

A few drops of Vanilla.

Method—

Wash the prunes and let them soak in the water for one hour. Then turn them into a saucepan with the water, and add the sugar and lemon juice. Stew them slowly until quite tender. When the prunes are soft, strain them and reserve the liquid. Stone the prunes, and cut each in four pieces. Return the liquid to the saucepan, and reduce it to form a sauce.

Put the yolks of eggs and sugar into a basin, and work them together with a wooden spoon until of a creamy consistency. Add the prunes and vanilla flavouring. Whip the whites to a stiff froth, and stir them lightly into the other mixture. Pour all into a greased pie-dish or fireproof dish, and bake in a moderate oven for about minutes. Serve it as soon as it is taken from the oven. Strain the liquid from the prunes into a sauce-boat, and serve it separately as a sauce.

If liked, a few chopped almonds or the kernels from the prunes may be added to the soufflé.

91.—SEMOLINA SOUFFLÉ.

Ingredients—

2 oz. Semolina.	3 yolks of Eggs.
1 pint Milk.	4 whites of Eggs.
2 oz. Castor Sugar.	A pinch of Salt.

Flavouring.

Method—

Rinse out a small stewpan with cold water, and put the semolina and milk into it. Stir over the fire with a wooden spoon until boiling, and then allow the semolina to simmer slowly for about ten minutes until it is well cooked. Then remove the pan from the fire, and add the sugar and any flavouring that is liked. Drop in the yolks one at a time, beating thoroughly between each. Put the whites of the eggs in a large basin, and with a wire whisk beat them up to a very stiff froth. With a metal spoon stir these lightly but thoroughly into the semolina mixture, and then pour all into a prepared soufflé tin (see page viii). Cover with greased paper, and steam slowly and steadily from thirty to forty minutes, or until the soufflé is well risen and feels firm to the touch. Turn out carefully on a hot dish, and serve with Jam, Custard, or any other suitable sauce poured round it.

92.—VANILLA SOUFFLÉ.

Ingredients—

1 oz. Butter.	3 yolks of Eggs.
1 oz. Flour.	4 whites of Eggs.
1 oz. Castor Sugar.	A pinch of Salt.
1 gill Milk.	Vanilla flavouring.

Method—

Melt the butter in a small stewpan, add the flour, and mix the two smoothly together with a wooden spoon, allowing them to cook for a few minutes without browning. Then add the milk, and stir over the fire until thoroughly cooked. When ready, the mixture will look smooth, and will draw away readily from the bottom and sides of the saucepan. This is called the panada. Remove the pan from the fire, and add the sugar and flavouring, or vanilla sugar may be used. Then add the yolks one at a time, beating the mixture

well between each. Put the whites into a large basin
or beating bowl, add a pinch of salt to them, and with
a wire whisk beat them up to a very stiff froth. Remove the wooden spoon from the mixture, and with an
iron one stir the beaten whites lightly but thoroughly
in. Pour this into a prepared soufflé tin (see page viii)
one and a half pint size, cover with greased paper,
and steam slowly and steadily from half to three-
quarters of an hour, or until the soufflé is well risen
and feels firm to the touch (see page ix). Turn out
carefully on to a hot dish, and serve *at once* with Jam,
Custard, Chocolate, or Wine Sauce poured round it.

93.—OMELET SOUFFLÉ.

Ingredients—

3 Eggs.	Grated rind of $\frac{1}{2}$ Lemon.
$1\frac{1}{2}$ oz. Sugar.	A little Jam.

Method—

Put the yolks into a basin with the sugar and grated
lemon rind or other flavouring, and mix well with a
wooden spoon until of a pale creamy consistency.
Whip the whites, with a pinch of salt added to them,
to a very stiff froth, and fold them very lightly into the
yolks. Do not stir more than is necessary. Pour the
mixture into a well-greased omelet pan, and put in a
brisk oven from seven to ten minutes until of a pale
brown colour. When firm to the touch, turn the
omelet out of the pan on to sugared paper, put a tablespoonful of warm jam in the centre, and fold over.
Lift the omelet on to a hot dish with a dish-paper, and
serve at once.

NOTES.—A little stewed fruit may be used instead of jam, or the omelet may be served plain.

A plain iron or copper pan is the best. If there is any danger of the omelet sticking to the pan, the foot of the pan may be lined first with a round of greased paper.

94.—(Another Way.)

If preferred, turn part of the mixture on to a flat dish, and with a knife shape it into a round with a depression in the centre. Put the rest into a forcing-bag, and press it out through a large pipe into lines or dots over the mound. Sprinkle with sugar, and bake in a good oven from ten to twelve minutes. Serve at once on the dish on which it is baked.

NOTE.—A little jam may be put in the centre before using the bag and pipe.

95.—CHOCOLATE OMELET.

Ingredients—

1½ to 2 oz. Chocolate.	3 Eggs.
2 tablespoonfuls Milk.	1 oz. Sugar.
1 dessertspoonful	1 oz. Butter.
Cream.	2 or 3 drops of Vanilla.

Method—

Cut the chocolate into small pieces, and dissolve it in a stewpan with the milk. It must be perfectly smooth and free from lumps. Remove the saucepan from the fire, and allow the chocolate to cool a little. Then add the yolks of eggs, cream, sugar, and vanilla, mix thoroughly for a few minutes, and lastly stir in the whites of eggs beaten to a stiff froth. Have the butter melted in an omelet or frying pan, and pour the chocolate mixture into it. Stir with a spoon for a minute or two, then allow the omelet to set over a moderate fire until brown on the under side. When ready, roll it up and sprinkle with sugar. Serve at once on a hot dish, with or without Chocolate Sauce poured round it (Recipe 115).

96.—RUM OMELET.

Make according to Recipe 93 or 94. Place the dish, holding the omelet on a second and larger dish to prevent accident from fire. When ready to place on the table, pour over the omelet a few spoonfuls of rum and light it.

97.—BATTER FOR FRITTERS.

Ingredients—

¼ lb. Flour.	1 tablespoonful Salad
1 gill tepid Water.	Oil or melted Butter.
2 or 3 whites of Eggs.	A pinch of Salt.

Method—

Sieve the flour and salt into a basin, and make a well in the centre. Add the water by degrees, and beat well with a wooden spoon to make a smooth paste free from lumps. Then add the oil or butter, and beat again for a few minutes. Whisk the whites of eggs to a stiff froth, and stir them in very lightly at the last.

NOTES.—This batter may be used for all kinds of fritters.

Sugar should not be added, as it is apt to make it heavy.

It is better if allowed to stand for some time before using, and before the whites of eggs are added.

A little rum or liqueur may be added if desired.

The batter should be very thick, and of the consistency to coat completely the article it is intended to cover.

98.—BATTER FOR FRITTERS.
(Another Way.)

Ingredients—

2 Eggs.	1 tablespoonful Brandy.
2 tablespoonfuls Salad Oil.	½ lb. Flour.
	A pinch of Salt.

1½ gills of light Beer.

Method—

Sieve the flour and salt into a basin, and make a well in the centre. Add the other ingredients by degrees, and mix well until perfectly smooth. If too thick, add a little tepid water. Cover the basin, and let the batter stand in a very cool place at least six hours before using.

99.—ALMOND FRITTERS.

Ingredients—

1 oz. Flour.	2 oz. ground Almonds.
½ pint Milk.	1 oz. Butter.
2 yolks of Eggs.	A pinch of Salt.

Egg and Bread-crumbs.

Method—

Add the milk gradually to the flour, and then stir them over the fire until boiling. Add the butter, ground almonds, sugar, salt, and yolks of eggs, and cook for a few minutes longer. Then spread the mixture on to a plate, and allow it to become quite cold. When firm, divide into small equal-sized pieces, and roll these upon a floured board into the shape of a cork. Egg and bread-crumb them, and fry to a nice colour in boiling fat. Drain well, and roll in powdered sugar. A little grated chocolate may be mixed with the sugar. Serve these piled up on a hot dish.

100.—AMERICAN FRITTERS OR DOUGHNUTS.

Ingredients—

2 Eggs.
4 tablespoonfuls melted Butter.
4 to 6 oz. Castor Sugar.
$\frac{1}{4}$ teaspoonful Salt.
$\frac{1}{2}$ pint Milk.

$\frac{1}{4}$ teaspoonful ground Cinnamon.
1 teaspoonful Baking Powder.
Flour to make a soft dough.

Method—

Sieve the sugar into a basin, and beat these two well together with a wooden spoon until light and creamy. Then add the butter melted, the cinnamon, salt, baking powder, and milk. Sieve in by degrees enough flour to make a soft light dough, and knead very gently for a few minutes. Flour the baking-board and rolling-pin, and roll the dough out one inch thick. Cut it into small circles or rings or strips, and twist them. Or the paste may be rolled out thinner, small rounds cut out, and two put together with a small

spoonful of jam between. Wet round the edge one
piece of pastry, and press the two edges well together.

Fry these fritters in boiling fat in the same manner
as for Beignets Soufflés (Recipe 103). Allow them to
cook rather slowly, and fry a golden brown. Drain
them on kitchen paper, and roll them in powdered
sugar while still warm.

101.—APPLE FRITTERS.

Required—

Frying Batter.	Sugar.
Apples.	Flavouring.

Method—

Choose firm ripe apples; rennets are best. Peel
three or four, and cut them in slices an eighth of an
inch in thickness. Then with a small round cutter
stamp out the cores. Put the apple rings on a plate,
and sprinkle them with orange or lemon sugar (84),
and if liked, a few drops of rum or brandy. Let
them soak for a few minutes, then steep a round of
apple in the batter. Coat it well, lift it out with a
skewer, and drop it into a saucepan of boiling fat.
Repeat this with the other rounds of apple, but do
not put more than six or seven pieces into the fat at
one time, as they swell considerably in the cooking.
Turn them over while in the fat, and let them fry
a nice amber colour. Lift them out with a skimmer
or perforated spoon, and dry on sugared paper in a
moderate oven until all are fried. Then serve them
on a folded serviette or dish-paper, the slices over-
lapping.

102.—BANANA FRITTERS.

Required—

3 or 4 Bananas. | Frying Batter (Recipe
Castor Sugar. | 97).

Wine or Lemon Juice.

Method—

Peel the bananas, cut them in two lengthways and then once across, making four pieces in all. Lay these pieces on a plate, sweeten and flavour, and let them lie for a few minutes. Finish off in the same way as Apple Fritters (Recipe 101).

103.—BEIGNETS SOUFFLÉS.

Ingredients—

5 oz. Flour. | 3 Eggs.
2 oz. Butter. | ½ pint Water.
1 oz. Castor Sugar. | Flavouring.

A pinch of Salt.

Method—

Put the water, butter, sugar, and salt into a stewpan, and bring them to the boil over the fire. Then draw the pan to the side of the fire, and add the flour which has been previously passed through a sieve. Mix all briskly with a spoon until it becomes a perfectly smooth paste. Stir this paste for a minute or two over a moderate fire, then remove the pan from the fire, and add the flavouring and one egg. Work the paste well until the egg is completely mixed in, then add the other two eggs one at a time, beating well between each. Let it stand till cold. When ready to serve, drop a spoonful at a time into hot fat,

and fry to an amber colour. Fry only a few at a time,
as more cools the fat too much, and also they require
room to swell. The paste will puff into hollow balls,
and increase three times in size. When ready, drain
well on sugared paper, and arrange in a pyramid on a
dish. Serve with Lemon or Orange Sauce (see
Sauces 119, 120).

104.—BREAD FRITTERS (Pain Perdu).

Ingredients—

4 or 5 slices of Bread.	2 oz. Butter.
½ pint Milk.	Castor Sugar.
1 Egg.	Some Jam.

Method—

Cut the bread from a tin loaf and half an inch in
thickness. Remove the crusts and cut each slice in
two. Place the bread in a dish and pour the milk
over. Allow it to soak until soft but not pappy.
Then brush each piece over with beaten egg. Melt
the butter in a frying pan, and fry the prepared bread
in it, cooking it until a golden brown colour on both
sides. Then drain on kitchen paper, and dredge well
with sugar. Keep the fritters hot until all are fried.
Arrange them in a circle on a hot dish, allowing one
to overlap the other slightly, and put a small teaspoonful of jam on each.

NOTE.—This dish may be varied by putting some
nicely stewed fruit in the centre of the dish instead of
jam. Then different flavourings may be added to the
milk used to soak the bread, or a little honey or syrup
may be heated and poured over the fritters at the last.

105.—CHERRY FRITTERS.

Required—

Cherries.
Angelica.
A little Kirsch or Wine.

Powdered Sugar.
Frying Batter (Recipe
97 or 98).

Method—

Stone the cherries, and put five or six at a time on to thin strips of angelica. (If the angelica is hard to cut, it ought to be soaked for a short time in hot water.) Sprinkle with sugar and a few drops of Kirsch or other liqueur or wine. Steep for a few minutes, then finish in the same way as Apple Fritters (Recipe 101).

106.—ORANGE FRITTERS.

Required—

2 or 3 Oranges.
Castor Sugar.

Frying Batter (Recipes
97 or 98).

Method—

Remove the peel and under white skin from the oranges. Divide them in six or eight pieces, but in a natural way, so that each piece retains its juice. Put them on a dish, and sprinkle with fine sugar; leave them for quarter of an hour, then drain. Dip each piece of orange in frying batter, coating it well, and drop it into boiling fat. Leave them until they have taken a nice brown colour, and drain them on kitchen paper sprinkled with sugar. Keep them warm in the oven until all are finished. Dish neatly on a d'oyley or dish-paper, and sprinkle a little orange sugar over. Serve very hot.

107.—PANCAKES.

Ingredients—

½ lb. Flour.	A little Lard for frying.
1 pint Milk.	Castor Sugar.
2 Eggs.	Lemon or Orange
A pinch of Salt.	Juice.

Method—

There are several kinds of batter for making pan-cakes. The above is one of the simplest.

Sieve the flour and salt into a basin, and make a well in the centre. Drop in the two yolks of eggs, and with a wooden spoon mix a little of the flour gradually into them. Then add about half the milk very gradually, mixing in the flour by degrees from the sides of the basin. Keep the batter thick enough to allow of all lumps being rubbed smooth, then beat well until it is full of air-bubbles. Add the rest of the milk, and if possible allow the batter to stand for an hour at least before using it. Just at the last stir in quickly and lightly the whites of the eggs beaten to a stiff froth.

Melt some lard in a saucepan, and let it stand by the side of the fire to keep warm. Put a little into a small frying or omelet pan, and make it smoking hot. Then pour quickly into the centre of the pan half a gill or so of batter. If the fat is hot enough, the batter will run all over the pan at once, whereas if it has not quite reached the required heat, the pan may have to be tilted a little to get the batter to cover it properly. Allow it to rest for a minute or two until set or nicely browned on the under side, then slip a broad-bladed knife round the edges, and then either toss the pancake over or turn it with the knife. Brown on the other side, then slip the pancake on to sugared paper, strew sugar over it, sprinkle with lemon or orange juice, and roll up. Keep this pancake hot on a plate placed over hot water until the rest are cooked. Each pancake will require a little fresh fat added to the pan. Serve them very hot, and as quickly as possible, and send cut lemon or orange to table with them.

NOTES.—For pancakes, choose a perfectly clean frying or omelet pan. If it is a new one, or one which has been out of use for some time, it ought to be *seasoned*, or the first pancake will be sure to stick. To do this, put some lard into the pan, and heat it until it begins to turn brown; then pour it away, and wipe the pan well with a soft cloth or with pieces of paper. Then add fresh lard to fry the pancake. A little salt heated in the pan is also a good thing for cleaning it. The pancakes may be made richer by adding more eggs to the batter, and keeping back some of the milk, or two ounces of butter melted may be added. They may be varied by spreading them with some nice jam before rolling them up, and sprinkling them with sugar, either plain or flavoured. Or they may be sprinkled pretty thickly with vanilla chocolate, one pancake put flat on the top of the other, leaving the last one plain, and served with cream.

Instead of milk, half beer and half tepid water may be used for mixing the batter, and a little rum or liqueur may be added.

108 —PEACH OR APRICOT FRITTERS.

Required—

Peaches or Apricots.	Castor Sugar.
Macaroon or Biscuit-crumbs.	Maraschino or other flavouring.

Frying Batter (97).

Method—

Cut the fruit in halves or quarters, and remove the stones. Sprinkle the pieces with sugar and a few drops of Maraschino, and roll them in macaroon or other biscuit-crumbs before dipping them in the batter. Finish in the same manner as Apple Fritters (101).

NOTE.—Tinned fruit does very well for these if it is drained.

109.—PEAR FRITTERS.

Required—

Good Pears.	Brandy or Liqueur.
Castor Sugar.	Frying Batter (98).

Method—

Take four or five good pears, peel them, and cut them in quarters. Take out the pips and core, and soak the pieces of pear for twenty minutes in a little liqueur or brandy and some castor sugar. Finish the same as for Apple Fritters (101).

110.—RICE CROQUETTES.

Ingredients—

3 oz. Carolina Rice.	The grated rind of 1 Lemon.
1 gill of cold Water.	
1 pint Milk.	2 yolks of Eggs.
A pinch of Salt.	1 whole Egg.
2 oz. Sugar.	Bread-crumbs.
1 oz. Butter.	A little Flour.

G

Method—

Wash the rice well in several waters, and then put it into a lined stewpan with the gill of fresh cold water. Bring this to the boil over the fire, cook for five minutes, and pour the water off. Then add the milk, butter, and grated lemon rind, and stew the rice slowly until quite soft and thick. From half to three-quarters of an hour will be necessary for this process. When ready, remove the pan from the fire, and stir in the yolks of eggs and sugar. Then turn the mixture on to a plate, smooth it over with a wetted knife, and set it aside to cool.

When cold, divide it into ten or twelve equal-sized pieces, place them on a board sprinkled with a little flour, and shape each one neatly either into balls, round flat cakes, cork or pear shapes. Then egg and bread-crumb them, and re-shape so as to take away the rough appearance. Fry these croquettes in a saucepan of boiling fat, until a golden brown colour, then drain them on paper and dredge with sugar. Serve them piled on a hot dish, with a dish-paper under them, and any suitable sauce may be served separately.

If the croquettes are in the form of a pear, a small piece of angelica may be stuck into the end of each to form the stalk.

III.—SEMOLINA FRITTERS.

Ingredients—

½ pint Milk.	2 oz. Currants.
3 oz. Semolina.	Flavouring.
1½ oz. Sugar.	½ oz. Butter.
1 whole Egg and 1 Yolk.	Egg and Bread-crumbs.

Method—

Put the semolina, milk, and butter into a saucepan, and stir them over the fire until thick. Then cook from eight to ten minutes. Remove the saucepan from the fire, and add the eggs, sugar, flavouring, and currants picked and cleaned. Mix well, and spread this mixture to the thickness of half an inch on a wetted dish or tin, and allow it to cool. When cold, cut out in small shapes with a cutter, egg and breadcrumb them, and fry in boiling fat to a beautiful brown colour.

NOTE.—The currants may be omitted, or preserved cherries or ginger cut in small pieces may be used in their place.

SAUCES.

Apricot Sauce.
Brandy Sauce (1).
Brandy Sauce (2).
Chocolate Sauce.
Custard Sauce.
Hard Sauce.
Jam Sauce.
Lemon Sauce.
Orange Sauce.
Pineapple Sauce.
Sauce au Liqueur.
Sauce Mousseline.
Strawberry Sauce.
Sweet White Sauce.
Wine Sauce (1).
Wine Sauce (2).
Whipped Raspberry Sauce.

112.—APRICOT SAUCE.

Ingredients—

1½ gills Apricot Purée.
½ oz. Arrowroot.
½ gill Water.
1 dessertspoonful Sugar.

2 or 3 drops of Carmine.
1 teaspoonful Maraschino or other flavouring.

Method—

Make the purée from tinned apricots by rubbing four or five pieces through a hair sieve and making up the quantity with the syrup. Put this purée into a small lined saucepan, add to it the arrowroot broken with the cold water, and stir over the fire until it boils and thickens. Add the sugar, flavouring, and enough carmine to make it a pretty pink colour. Cook two or three minutes longer, and serve.

113.—BRANDY SAUCE (1).

Ingredients—

1 oz. Butter	1 oz. Sugar.
½ oz. Flour.	1½ gills Water.

½ glass Brandy.

Method—

Melt the butter in a small lined saucepan, add the flour, and mix with a wooden spoon until smooth. Draw the pan to one side, and pour in the water; then return to the fire and stir constantly until boiling. Add the brandy and sugar, and boil a few minutes longer.

114.—BRANDY SAUCE (2).

Ingredients—

2 yolks of Eggs.	½ gill Water.
½ gill Cream.	½ glass of Brandy.

1 oz. Sugar.

Method—

Put all the ingredients into a basin, and stand the basin in a saucepan of slowly simmering water. Whisk the contents with a fork or small wire whisk from six to eight minutes until thick and frothy, when the sauce will be ready. Do not boil, or it will curdle.

115.—CHOCOLATE SAUCE.

Ingredients—

1 gill Milk.
1 oz. Chocolate.
1 teaspoonful Sugar.

1 yolk of Egg.
4 or 5 drops of Vanilla Essence.

Method—

Rinse out a small lined saucepan with cold water, and put into it the milk and chocolate, either grated or shred down finely with a knife. Simmer until quite dissolved. Mix the yolk of egg and sugar together in a basin, and pour the chocolate gradually on to them. Return to the saucepan, and stir over the fire until *almost* boiling. Remove at once, and add the flavouring.

116.—CUSTARD SAUCE.

Ingredients—

2 yolks of Eggs.
1 white of Egg.
½ pint Milk.

1 dessertspoonful Sugar.
A few drops of Flavouring.

Method—

Rinse out a small lined saucepan with cold water, put the milk into it, and let it heat over the fire. Put the yolks and white of egg into a basin with the sugar, and mix them well together with a wooden spoon. Then pour the hot milk gradually on to them, stirring all the time, and mix thoroughly. Return all to the saucepan, and stir very carefully over the fire until the sauce thickens. On no account must it be allowed to boil, or it will curdle. Have ready at hand a clean basin and a strainer. As soon as the sauce shows signs of thickening, and it is *almost* boiling, remove the pan from the fire, continue stirring for a second or two, then strain into the basin. Add flavouring to taste. To keep the sauce warm, stand the basin containing it in a saucepan of hot, not boiling water.

NOTE.—The sauce may be made richer by using more yolks of eggs and no whites.

117.—HARD SAUCE.

Ingredients—

2 oz. Fresh Butter.	A few drops of Vanilla
4 oz. Castor Sugar.	or 1 dessertspoonful
2 whites of Eggs.	Brandy, Sherry, or
	Liqueur.

Method—

Warm the butter very slightly in a basin, but be careful not to oil it. Sieve the sugar over it, and beat these two together with a wooden spoon until they are very white and light. Then add the whites of egg whipped to a stiff froth, and beat again for a few minutes. Flavour to taste, and set the sauce in a cool place or on ice to harden. Serve as cold as possible.

118.—JAM SAUCE.

Ingredients—

2 tablespoonfuls Red Jam.	A squeeze of Lemon Juice.
1 gill of Water.	2 or 3 drops of Carmine.
1 oz. Loaf Sugar.	

Method—

Put the water, sugar, and jam into a small lined saucepan, and let them boil quickly for a few minutes, skimming if necessary. Add the lemon juice and two or three drops of carmine. Strain before using.

NOTES.—Raspberry or strawberry jam is to be preferred for making this sauce.

A little wine may be added.

119.—LEMON SAUCE.

Ingredients—

½ oz. Arrowroot.	1 oz. Sugar.
Rind and juice of ½ Lemon.	1½ gills Water.
	½ oz. Butter.

Method—

Wipe the lemon with a damp cloth, and grate off half the rind on to the top of the sugar. Grate very lightly, being most particular not to take any of the white, as it is bitter. Work the lemon rind and sugar together until they are well blended. Break the arrowroot with a little of the water, then add the rest of the water, and pour into a saucepan. Stir over the fire until boiling, add the lemon, sugar, and the lemon juice strained, and cook for a few minutes. Break the butter in small pieces, and put it in just before serving.

120.—ORANGE SAUCE.

Ingredients—

½ oz. Arrowroot.	Juice of 1 Orange.
1 oz. Sugar.	2 tablespoonfuls Water.

Method—

Squeeze and strain the orange juice into a saucepan.
Break the arrowroot with the water, and add it to the
orange juice. Stir these over the fire until boiling,
then boil for a few minutes, and add the sugar. If too
thick, a little more orange juice may be added. Strain
before using.

121.—PINEAPPLE SAUCE.

Ingredients—

½ gill Pineapple Syrup.
2 oz. Pineapple.
½ oz. Sugar.
A few drops of Carmine.

2 tablespoonfuls Water
or Wine.
A squeeze of Lemon
Juice.

Method—

Strain the pineapple syrup into a small saucepan,
and add all the other ingredients. Boil for a few
minutes, and remove any scum that rises.

122.—SAUCE AU LIQUEUR.

(Sweet Sauce with Liqueur.)

Ingredients—

1 oz. Butter.
½ oz. Flour.
1 oz. Sugar.
1 yolk of Egg.
1 gill of Milk.

A few drops of Vanilla.
1 tablespoonful Red
Curaçoa.
½ oz. preserved Cherries.
½ oz. Pistachio Nuts.

Method—

Melt the butter in a small saucepan, add the flour,
and mix until smooth. Then draw the pan aside and

pour in the milk. Stir well over the fire until boiling. Add the sugar, yolk of egg, and vanilla, mix well, and add lastly the curaçoa and the pistachios and cherries both chopped.

123.—SAUCE MOUSSELINE.

Ingredients—

½ gill of Cream.	1½ oz. Castor Sugar.
3 yolks of Eggs.	1 tablespoonful Mara-
2 whites of Eggs.	schino.

Method—

Put all the ingredients into a basin, and stand the basin in a stewpan of slowly simmering water. Beat the contents with a fork or small whisk until they are thick and creamy, but do not allow them to boil. Serve at once.

124.—STRAWBERRY SAUCE.

Ingredients—

2 oz. Fresh Butter.	¼ lb. fresh Strawberries.
4 oz. Castor Sugar.	2 or 3 drops of Car-
1 white of Egg.	mine.

Method—

Make this sauce according to directions given for Hard Sauce (Recipe 117), and add the strawberries mashed to a pulp.

125.—SWEET WHITE SAUCE.

Ingredients—

1 oz. Butter.	1 dessertspoonful of
½ oz. Flour.	Sugar.
½ pint Milk.	A little Flavouring.

Method—

Melt the butter in a small saucepan, and be careful it does not discolour. Add the flour, mix it in with a wooden spoon, and allow the butter and flour to cook for a minute or two over the fire. Then draw the pan to one side, and pour in the milk. Stir again over the fire until the sauce boils and thickens, and simmer slowly for five or six minutes, so as to thoroughly cook the flour. Add the sugar, and flavour according to taste.

126.—WINE SAUCE (1).

Ingredients—

½ oz. Flour. | 1 oz. Sugar.
1 oz. Butter. | 1½ gills Water.
½ gill Sherry.

Method—

Melt the butter in a small lined saucepan, add the flour, and mix until smooth with a wooden spoon. Draw the pan to the side of the fire, and pour in the water. Then return the pan to the fire, and stir constantly until boiling. Add the wine and sugar, and boil two or three minutes longer.

127.—WINE SAUCE (2).

Ingredients—

2 yolks of Eggs. | 1 wine-glassful of
1 dessertspoonful of | Sherry.
Sugar. | 1 tablespoonful Cream.

Method—

Put all the ingredients into a basin, and stand the basin in a saucepan of slowly simmering water. Whisk the contents with a fork or small wire whisk until thick and frothy, and serve at once. Do not boil, or it will curdle.

128.—WHIPPED RASPBERRY SAUCE.

Ingredients—

2 tablespoonfuls Raspberry Syrup.
2 tablespoonfuls Water.

2 yolks of Eggs.
2 or 3 drops of Carmine.

Method—

Put all the ingredients into a basin, and stand the basin in a saucepan of slowly simmering water. Beat the contents with a fork or small wire whisk until thick and frothy, and serve at once.

NOTE.—Any other fruit syrup may be used in the same way.

INDEX.

---

www.ingramcontent.com/pod-product-compliance
Lightning Source LLC
Chambersburg PA
CBHW011800040426
42448CB00017B/3320